ORIGAMI
FOR HER

ORIGAMI
FOR HER

Didier Boursin

David and Charles

www.stitchcraftcreate.co.uk

Acknowledgements
I would first like to thank all those who, from near or far, helped me to develop the origami within this book.
Thank you to Olivier Ploton for the photos
Thank you to Élodie Pichon for her choice of beautiful papers
Thank you to Laureline Sibille for the corrections
Thank you to Nina and Angelo for their advice
Thank you to Setsuko for his good humour
And thank you to the entire editorial team
The publisher would also like to thank Linda-Laure Greff for her Kokeshi dolls illustrations on p. 60.

A DAVID & CHARLES BOOK
© Dessain et Tolra/Larousse 2011

Originally published in France as *Drôles d'Origamis Pour Les Filles*
First published in the UK and USA in 2013 by F&W Media International, Ltd

David & Charles is an imprint of F&W Media International, Ltd
Brunel House, Forde Close, Newton Abbot, TQ12 4PU, UK

F&W Media International, Ltd is a subsidiary of F+W Media, Inc
10151 Carver Road, Suite #200, Blue Ash, OH 45242, USA

A catalogue record for this book is available from the British Library.

ISBN-13: 978-1-4463-0352-8 paperback
ISBN-10: 1-4463-0352-7 paperback

Printed in China by RR Donnelley for:
F&W Media International, Ltd
Brunel House, Forde Close, Newton Abbot, TQ12 4PU, UK

10 9 8 7 6 5 4 3 2 1

Direction and editorial coordination: Colette Hanicotte
assisted by Élodie Pichon and Laureline Sibille
Editing: Henri Goldszal, Joëlle Narjollet
Graphic design: Either
Layout: ELSE
Photographs: Olivier Ploton
Cover: Véronique Laporte/Suzan Pak Poy
Production: Anne Raynaud

Photographic credits for the decorated papers:
p. 2, p. 57, p. 65, p. 215, p. 217 © Oowenoc - Fotolia.com; p. 6 © Keekeekee - Fotolia.com; p. 6, p. 9, p. 17, p. 22, p. 127, p. 129 © Smilewithjul - Fotolia.com; p. 6, p. 17, p. 24, p. 131, p. 133 © Stasys Eidiejus - Fotolia.com; p. 38, p. 153, p. 155 © Smilewithjul - Fotolia.com; p. 6, p. 9, p. 26, p. 135, p. 136, p. 137, p. 138 © Polina Katritch - Fotolia.com; p. 6, p. 17, p. 20, p. 123, p. 125 © L.Bouvier - Fotolia.com; p. 6, p. 42, p. 161, p. 163 © Vman - Fotolia.com; p. 7, p. 77, p. 243, p. 245, p. 247, p. 249 © DOGGYTEAM - Fotolia.com; p. 7, p. 106, p. 319, p. 321 © Alexstar - Fotolia.com; p. 86, p. 267, p. 269, p. 271, p. 273 © Nataliya Dolotko - Fotolia.com; p. 16, p. 28, p. 139, p. 141, p. 143, p. 145 © Ihor-seamless - Fotolia.com; p. 18, p. 121 © LenLis - Fotolia.com; p. 31, p. 147 © Arhangelskij - Fotolia.com; p. 34, p. 54, p. 189, p. 190, p. 191, p. 192, p. 193, p. 194, p. 195, p. 196, p. 197, p. 198, p. 199, p. 200, p. 201, p. 202 © Sergey Titov - Fotolia.com; p. 36, p. 149, p. 151 © Komvell - Fotolia.com; p. 38, p. 157, p. 159 © OMKAR A.V - Fotolia.com; p. 44, p. 165, p. 167 © Ultramarin - Fotolia.com; p. 44, p. 169, p. 171 © Dmitry Remesov - Fotolia.com; p. 46, p. 173, p. 175 © Rada Covalenco - Fotolia.com; p. 48, p. 177, p. 179 © Svetlana Prokhorova - Fotolia.com; p. 48, p. 178, p. 180 © Stasys Eidiejus - Fotolia.com; p. 50, p. 181, p. 183 © Notkoo2008 - Fotolia.com; p. 9, p. 35, p. 52, p. 185, p. 187 © Nataliya Dolotko - Fotolia.com; p. 56, p. 235, p. 237 © Polina Katritch - Fotolia.com; p. 58, p. 203, p. 205 © Susanne Karlsson - Fotolia.com; p. 74, p. 60, p. 207 © Galina Pankratova - Fotolia.com; p. 62, p. 209, p. 211, p. 213 © Sandra Willauer - Fotolia.com; p. 68, p. 219, p. 221, p. 223 © Printing Society - Fotolia.com; p. 68, p. 225, p. 227 © Notkoo2008 - Fotolia.com; p. 70, p. 229, p. 231, p. 233 © Arrows - Fotolia.com; p. 74, p. 76, p. 239 © Richard Laschon - Fotolia.com; p. 74, p. 241 © Elena Kravchuk - Fotolia.com; p. 79, p. 251, p. 253, p. 255 © Anna Tchekhovitch - Fotolia.com; p. 82, p. 257, p. 259 © Susanne Karlsson - Fotolia.com; p. 84, p. 261, p. 263, p. 265 © Cyrinne - Fotolia.com; p. 89, p. 275, p. 277, p. 279, p. 281, p. 283, p. 285, p. 287, p. 289, p. 291 © Emaria - Fotolia.com; p. 94, p. 293, p. 295 © Uclapucla - Fotolia.com; p. 96, p. 297, p. 299, p. 301 © Ihor-seamless - Fotolia.com; p. 98, p. 303 © Myrtille MLB - Fotolia.com; p. 100, p. 307, p. 309 © Elena Show - Fotolia.com; p. 100, p. 311, p. 313 © Nobilior - Fotolia.com; p. 103, p. 105, p. 315, p. 317 © Inna - Fotolia.com; p. 108, p. 323, p. 325 © Ihor-seamless - Fotolia.com; p. 110, p. 327 © Konovalov Pavel - Fotolia.com; p. 112, p. 329, p. 331 © Roman Sigaev - Fotolia.com; p. 112, p. 333 © Emaria - Fotolia.com; p. 115, p. 335 © Eka Panova - Fotolia.com; p. 115, p. 337, p. 339 © LenLis - Fotolia.com; p. 118, p. 341, p. 343 © Cristi180884 - Fotolia.com; p. 118, p. 342, p. 344 © Tasia12 - Fotolia.com; stickers p. 346, p. 348 © Itiho - Fotolia.com, © RADIANT - Fotolia.com, © Rubysoho - Fotolia.com, © Beaubelle - Fotolia.com, © Elena Kravchuk - Fotolia.com, © Amy Lau - Fotolia.com, © Aalto - Fotolia.com, © Ekaterina Voinova - Fotolia.com, © Jaeeho - Fotolia.com, © HPPhoto - Fotolia.com, © Ntnt - Fotolia.com

F+W Media publishes high quality books on a wide range of subjects.
For more great book ideas visit: www.stitchcraftcreate.co.uk

Foreword

Origami, with its universal language of fold symbols, is popular around the world. The growing interest in this art form is largely due to a handful of creative people who have succeeded in breathing new life into traditional themes. With this aim in mind, I have created a variety of paper folded models for you to choose from. There is a collection of ephemeral jewellery, from earrings and necklaces to brooches and bracelets, made with pretty papers. Or you may prefer to decorate your home by making small boxes and decorations, from practical dishes and vases to beautiful flowers and garlands. Or why not choose from the gifts and messges to make models that are a little out of the ordinary. Whatever you choose to make, these small contemporary sculptures, with their limited requirements and simple and precise moves, allow me to let you into a universe that I have created. Each and every fold has been carefully thought out and designed to ensure your maximum enjoyment. Have fun choosing your papers and conjuring up these creations. Origami is a transient art form that encourages reflection and promotes a zen-like mood. Enjoy the time you spend creating these unusual origami models and share them with your friends.

Didier Boursin

Contents

Earrings and necklaces

Brooches and bracelets

Boxes and decorations

Gifts and messages

Materials

Very few materials are required to start folding your own jewellery. You are likely to have most requirements to hand: a pair of scissors, a glue stick, super glue, sticky tape. You will also need:

Metal eye pins: gold or silver. Thread origami creations and beads onto these to form earrings and pendants.

Jump rings: gold or silver. These are used to mount earrings or pendants.

Crimping beads: small metal beads. Use a small pair of pliers to crimp these to metal eye pins to lock beads and origami creations in place.

Brooch pins

Earring findings: gold or silver. Attach these small hooks to jump rings to mount earrings.

Beads

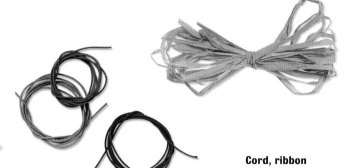

Cord, ribbon

Jewellery mounting

Mounting equipment:
Mounting the various items of jewellery is simple enough, but there are a few pieces of essential equipment you will need.

Needles: in order to pierce holes for jump rings and earring findings.

Glue: to attach brooch clips and metal eye pins, or to glue certain folds in place.

Round-nose pliers: to open jump rings or earring findings, or to bend metal eye pins; also used for closing crimping beads.

Wire cutters: to shorten metal eye pins.

Mounting an earring or pendant using a jump ring:
• Simply pierce a hole in your origami, not too close to the edge and large enough to insert a jump ring. Use round-nose pliers to gently open the ring and close it back up again. If the origami is to be made into an earring, insert an earring finding into the jump ring. It is best to do this before attaching the origami to the finding.

Mounting an earring using a metal eye pin:

· **With crimping bead:** thread the metal eye pin through the top of the origami so that the loop is at the top of the model. Thread on a bead below the origami, then a crimping bead. Using a small pair of pliers, close the crimping bead in order to fix everything in place.

· **Without crimping bead:** insert the metal eye pin through the underside of the origami (so that the loop is at the bottom). If you wish you can thread on a bead or a pearl before inserting the eye pin through the origami. Using a pair of pliers, form a small loop at the other end of the eye pin (top of the model). This will then be attached to an earring finding. If the eye pin is too long use a pair of wire cutters to cut it to size.

Mounting a brooch using a finding:
• Simply glue the brooch finding to the back of the origami using strong glue. Use a small tab of cardboard and a small brush to put on the right amount of glue.

Preserving origami models:
You can use a clear, water-based varnish or nail polish to coat your origami models to seal and protect small accessories and jewellery items.

Folds and symbols
> Advice

Before starting, take a moment to read through Folds and symbols (pp. 10–13) and Base shapes (pp. 14–15), which explain the basic folds. These include the 'valley' fold (folded inwards and crease is at the bottom) and the 'mountain' fold (folded outwards and crease is at the top), as well as other moves and fold combinations that will come in handy.

Each fold and movement is indicated in a diagram using an arrow and two joining dots. To avoid any mistakes, make sure you know the difference between 'folding the paper' and 'marking the fold'. In the first instance, you fold the paper and keep it folded; in the second, you simply mark the fold as indicated by the double-headed arrow. If necessary refer to the subsequent diagram; this should help you to understand the previous step.

When starting out, practise making basic models, starting from a square base, using ordinary paper. The best papers to use are those that are no more than 90g in weight. Once you've had some practise, you can move on to create any of the models using the papers recommended at the end of book. You will find that the random way in which the patterns meet the folds allows for the models to be created slightly differently each time.

The shaded diamonds indicate the difficulty level of the origami model; the more shaded diamonds, the more difficult it will be to fold. Start with the very easy models to get used to the symbols and to perfect the delicate folds and movements. Your first attempt may not be successful, but don't be discouraged; your second go is often better and paper is provided to make two versions of each model. Use one full sheet of the recommended paper unless otherwise indicated.

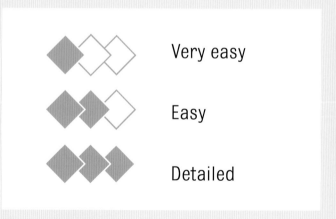

Very easy

Easy

Detailed

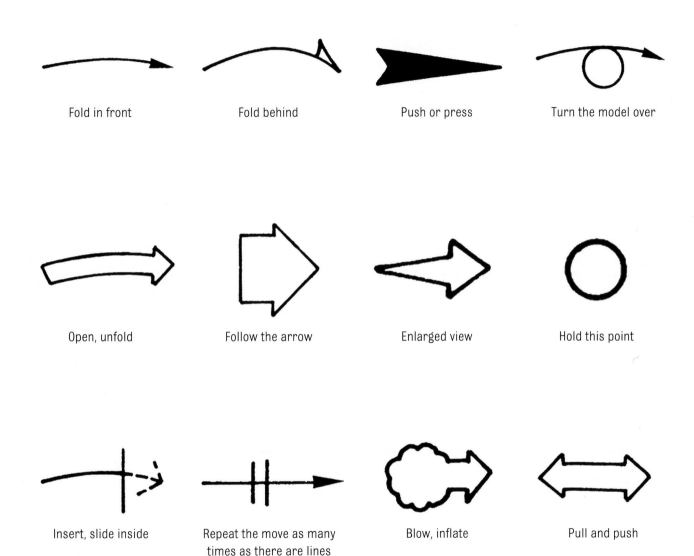

Fold in front

Fold behind

Push or press

Turn the model over

Open, unfold

Follow the arrow

Enlarged view

Hold this point

Insert, slide inside

Repeat the move as many
times as there are lines

Blow, inflate

Pull and push

Folds and symbols

> Basic folds

> Valley fold

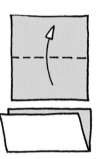

> Mountain fold

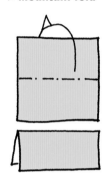

> Mark the fold

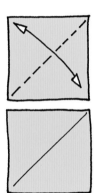

> Pleat or zigzag

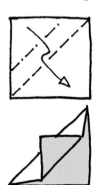

> Join the dots

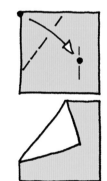

> Cut

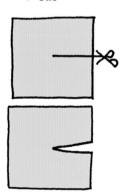

> Inside inverted fold

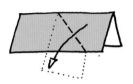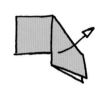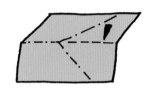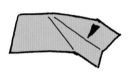

> Outside inverted fold

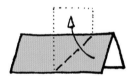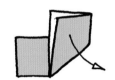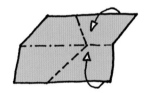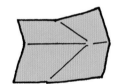

> Fold in thirds

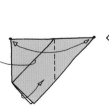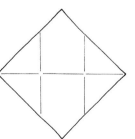

Base shapes

> Preliminary base

   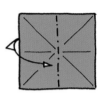

By pressing with your finger at the centre **(a)**, you obtain the Waterbomb base.

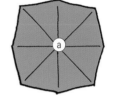  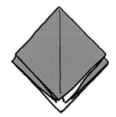

> Waterbomb base

  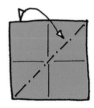 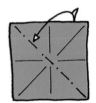

By pressing with your finger at the centre **(b)**, you obtain the Preliminary base.

 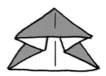 

> Diamond base

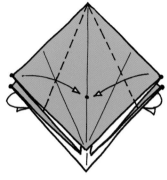

1. Fold the upper edges onto the two sides of a preliminary base.

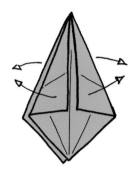

2. Unfold.

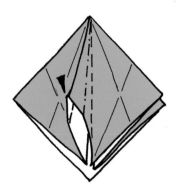

3. Lift up a flap vertically and then open by pressing to flatten.

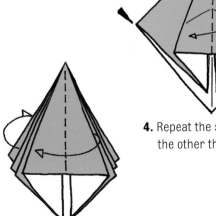

5. Turn one layer to the left on opposite sides.

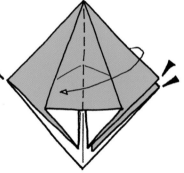

4. Repeat the same fold on the other three flaps.

Earrings and necklaces

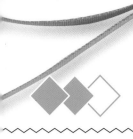

Love charm

A small book filled with sweet words.

For recommended paper, see p. 121
Cut an 8cm (3⅛in) square as marked on reverse

1 **Cut** the square in half to give you two rectangles

To make the book pages

2 **Mark** the centre fold on one of the paper rectangles

3 **Fold** in half from left to right

4 **On the back,** fold in half; on the front, mark the centre fold and unfold

5 **Make a cut** in the folded layers as shown and then fold in half backwards

To make the cover

6a **Fold in** the top and bottom edges of the second paper rectangle leaving a gap in the centre

6b **Fold** in half

6c **Fold each** side in half towards the centre fold

To assemble the book

7 **Slot** the end pages inside the cover flaps and glue

8 **To finish** the pendant, pierce a small hole in a corner of the cover and insert a jump ring

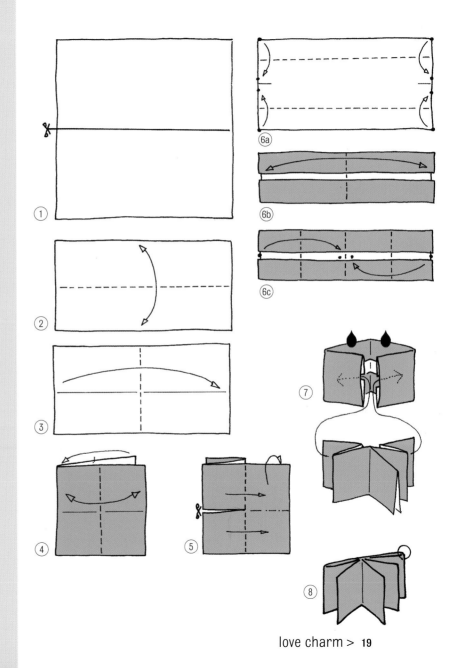

Twirling leaves

Adorn your ears with these pretty little leaves.

For recommended paper, see pp. 123 and 125
Cut an 8cm (3⅛in) square per earring as marked on reverse

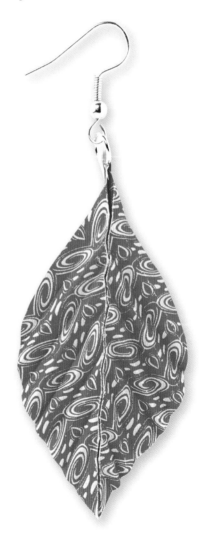

1. **Fold** the square in half

2. **Cut** a half leaf shape along the folded edge as shown

3. **Fold** one half to form the central vein

4. **Fold** the half on the other side of the central vein backwards

5. **Make** narrow accordion folds from the central vein, pressing down firmly

6. **Open** the leaf carefully and insert the tip of the central vein into a jump ring. Fold over the tip of the central vein and glue closed. Attach an earring finding to the jump ring

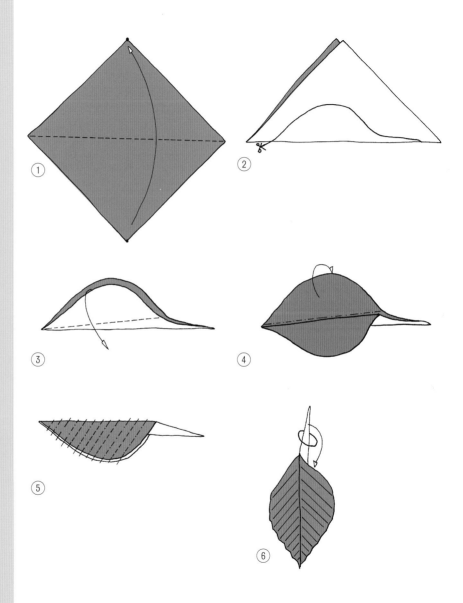

Diamond earrings

Inspired by large facet-cut diamonds, these earrings are so lightweight and colourful.

For recommended paper, see pp. 127 and 129
Cut an 8cm (3⅛in) square per earring as marked on reverse

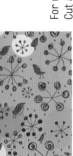

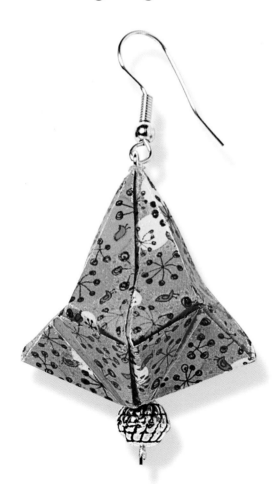

1. **Make** a diamond base (see p. 15) then fold the bottom tip up towards the left, joining the dots

2. **Unfold**, then repeat on the opposite side and unfold

3. **Fold in** the two sides, joining the dots

Details

4. **Refold** the square

5. **Slot** the triangle between the layers and glue

6. **Fold** the triangle over to the right

7. **Slot** the other part of the square between the layers and glue

8. **Turn** the sides, one by one, and repeat steps 3 to 6 on the remaining three sides

9. **Mark** the folds along the layers and then inflate

10. **To form** the diamond, press each side

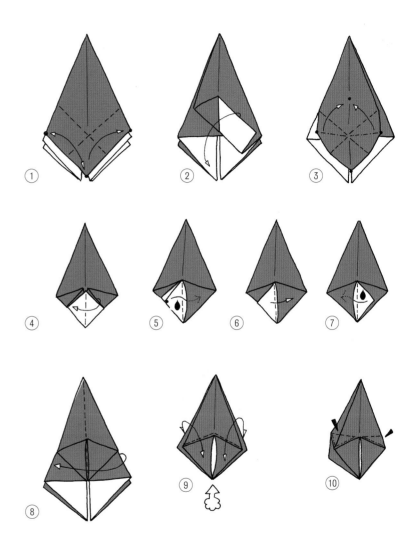

Little fishes

So easy to fold, yet these small fish-shaped earrings are such fun to wear.

For recommended paper, see pp. 131 and 133
Cut an 8cm (3⅛in) square per pair of earrings
as marked on reverse

1. **Cut** the square in half to give you two rectangles, one for each earring. Fold each rectangle to join the dots

2. **Fold** in half to join the dots as shown

3. **Check** your model is as shown, then unfold completely

4. **Refold** along the diagonal

5. **Fold** to the dots on both sides

6. **Fold in** each side between the layers

7. **Fold** one tip forward and the other back

8. **Fold** both tips towards the centre

9. **To lock in place**, cross the two tips

   Attach a jump ring, piercing through all the layers, then add an earring finding

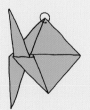

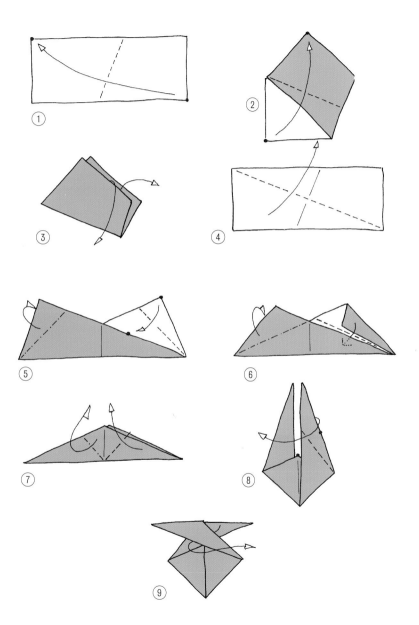

Psychedelic hoops

Go for a Sixties look with these funky coloured, psychedelic-patterned hoops.

For recommended paper, see pp. 135 and 137
Cut seven 4cm (1½in) squares per earring

1 **Take** one square of paper and fold in half

2 **Fold** one side along the diagonal

3 **Fold** the other side backwards. Make a total of seven units for each earring following steps 1 to 3

4 **Slide** two units into each other

5 **Fold** the tips inside the layers to fasten.

6 **Add** on the remaining five units to complete the ring

Pierce the edge of one corner to attach a jump ring and mount to an earring finding

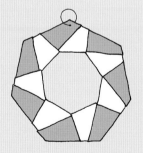

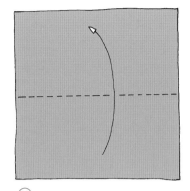

① ②

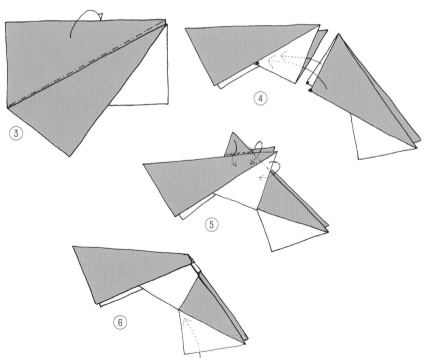

③ ④ ⑤ ⑥

Pyramid bead necklace

Made from either one sheet of the large or small patterned paper supplied, these chunky pyramid-shaped beads make quite an impact.

For recommended paper, see pp. 139, 141, 143 and 145

1 **Fold** a square of paper in half

2 **Fold** into thirds (see p. 13)

3 **Mark** the folds as shown, then
   unfold completely

4 **Pinch** the sides along the folds marked,
   then push in the central square to fold
   the whole thing flat

5 **Fold** as shown

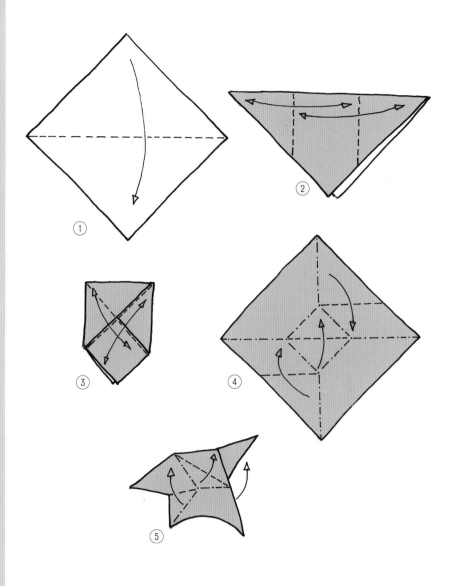

pyramid bead necklace > **29**

6 **Fold** the top and side tips as shown

7 **Slot** the triangle between the layers, then turn over

8 **Repeat** the top and side tip folds as before

9 **Slot** in the triangle, as before

10 **Pop up** the bead by gently pressing the ends between your thumb and index finger

11 **To make a necklace**, use a long needle to thread several pyramid beads onto a length of cord

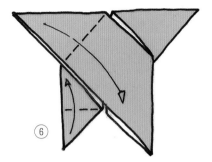

(6)

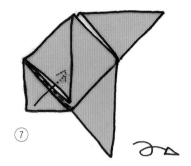

(7)

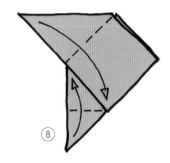

(8)

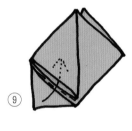

(9)

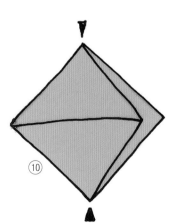

(10)

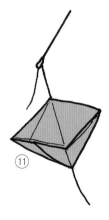

(11)

Medallion pendant

Folded from a small square of paper, this bright medallion is simply strung on a leather thong.

For recommended paper, see p. 147
Cut an 8cm (3⅛in) square

1 **Mark** the diagonal folds

2 **Fold** one side along the diagonal as shown

3 **Fold** the second side as in the previous step

4 **Fold** the third side

5 **Fold** the final side, joining the dots, then unfold

6 **Slot** the right-hand side inside, reversing the folds

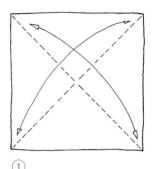

①

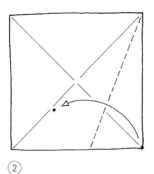

②

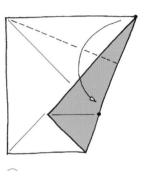

③

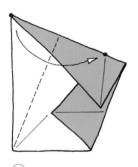

④

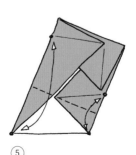

⑤

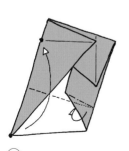

⑥

7 **Check** your model is as shown, then open up one tip

8 **Open** a second tip

9 **Open** a third tip

10 **Open** the last tip

11 **Slot** each tip inside (see below)

Pierce a small hole so you can insert a jump ring to slide a thin cord through to make a pendant

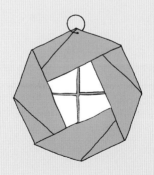

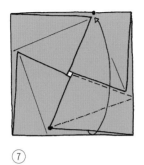

⑦

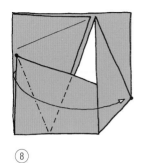

⑧

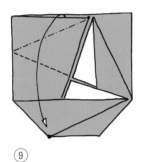

⑨

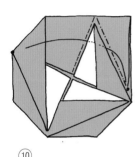

⑩

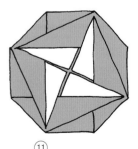

⑪

Brooches and bracelets

Little kitty badge

A cute little brooch in the shape of a cat's face.

For recommended paper, see pp. 149 and 151
Cut a 10cm (4in) square as marked on reverse

1. **Fold** a square in half

2. **Fold down** the sides and then fold up the left tip

3. **Fold up** the right tip, then fold in the small triangle to the left

4. **Fold in** the small triangle to the right. Push down the top part to form the head as shown. Fold up the top layer only at the base to join the dots

5. **Fold under** as shown, then turn the whole thing over

6. **Fold under** the bottom tip and then fold up the top layer only

7. **To finish the nose** fold as shown, then fold under the tip of the triangle at the base to complete the cat's face

   Attach a brooch pin to the back to complete

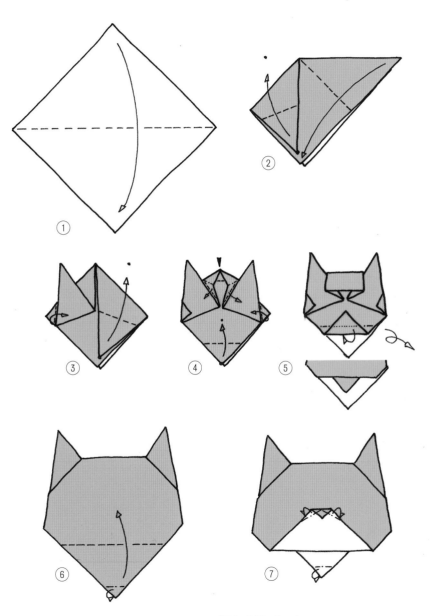

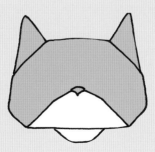

little kitty badge > 37

Star brooch

Two units, folded from matching or complementary papers, are joined together to make this eight-pointed star.

For recommended paper, see pp. 153, 155, 157 and 159
Cut two 10cm (4in) squares as marked on reverse

1 **Make** a preliminary base (see p. 14)

2 **Fold in** the sides of each face

3 **Fold down** the top to join the dots

4 **Unfold** the sides

5 **Mark** the folds in line with the triangle and then unfold the triangle

6 **Open** the sides out, holding where shown

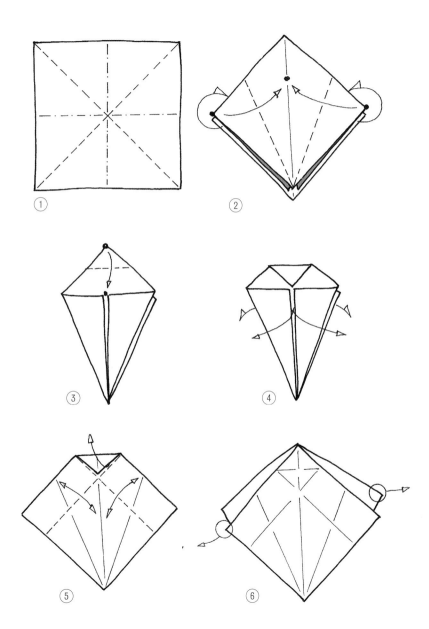

7 **Press** the centre to form the square

8 **Make** a fold on each side as shown

9 **Fold down** the upper part and open up the back

10 **Fold along** the lines shown, joining the dots

11 **Repeat** on the other three sides

12 **Make** another star in the same way

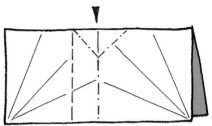

(7)

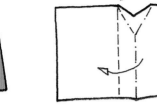

(8)

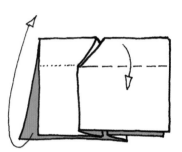

(9)

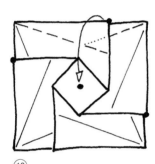

(10)

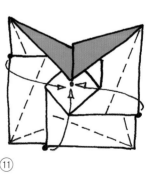

(11)

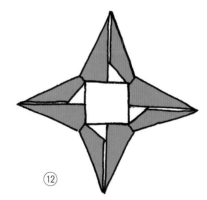

(12)

13 **Join** the two stars by sliding the inside ends of one onto the central square of the other

14 **Stick** a brooch pin to the back to finish

Variations

15 **Make** one simple star by folding in the centre as shown

16 **Check** your model is as shown, then fix a brooch pin to the back

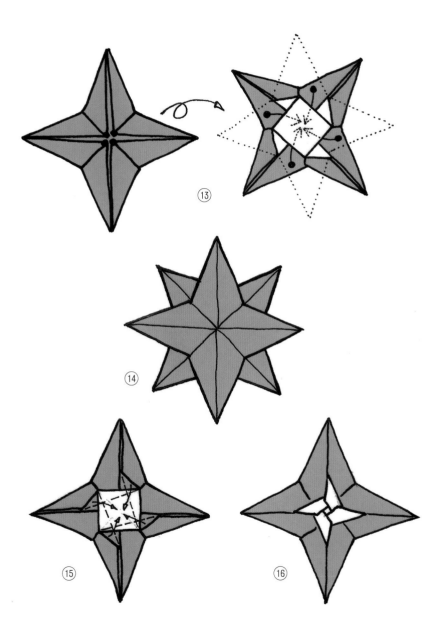

Butterfly bracelet

The ends of this expertly-made bracelet slot into each other neatly for ease of wearing.

For recommended paper, see pp. 161 and 163
Cut two strips 2.4cm (1in) wide as marked on reverse

1 **Cut** two strips

2 **Fold in** the corners of each end

3 **Mark** the folds on each strip as shown, joining the dots

4 **Mark** the other two folds on each strip as shown, then turn over

5 **Fold up** the ends

6 **Unfold**

7 **Fold** the ends along the fold lines shown

8 **Check** your model is as shown, then turn over

9 **Fold** the triangles, joining the dots

10 **Repeat** steps 3 to 9 to make a second diamond at each end

11 **Join** the folded bands together as shown, and glue in place

To close the bracelet, slide one end into the other and then fold down the triangles. Extra layers can be added inside to strengthen it

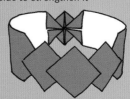

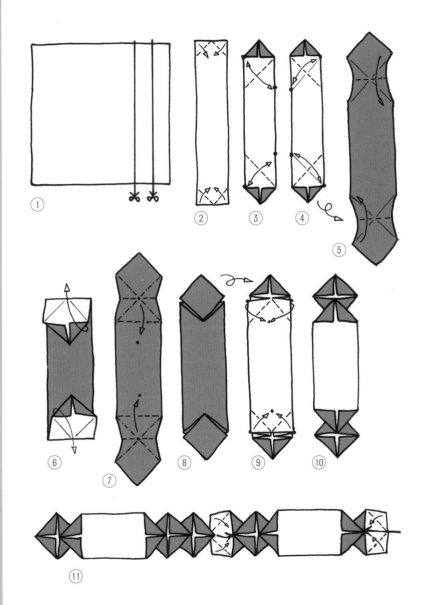

butterfly bracelet > **43**

Zigzag bangle

This beautiful paper latticework bracelet can be adapted to fit the size of your wrist.

For recommended paper, see pp. 165, 167, 169 and 171
Cut six strips 1.4cm (⁹⁄₁₆in) wide as marked on reverse

1. **Fold down** the top corner of each strip as shown

2. **Fold up** the strip along the edge of the triangle and then unfold

3. **Fold** the strip as shown and then turn over

4. **Repeat** by folding to the left, then to the right

5. **Repeat** the folding pattern to the end

6. **Glue** three strips together, adjusting the length as desired, to give you two long strips

7. **Weave** the two long strips together, in, out

8. **Close** the ends with glue

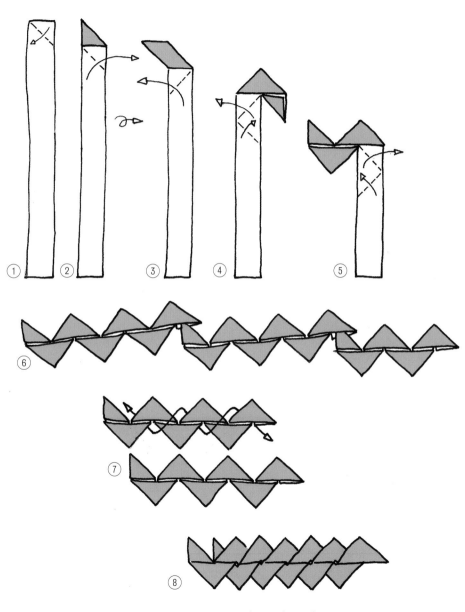

Pencil badge

This pencil-shaped pin will brighten up any outfit.

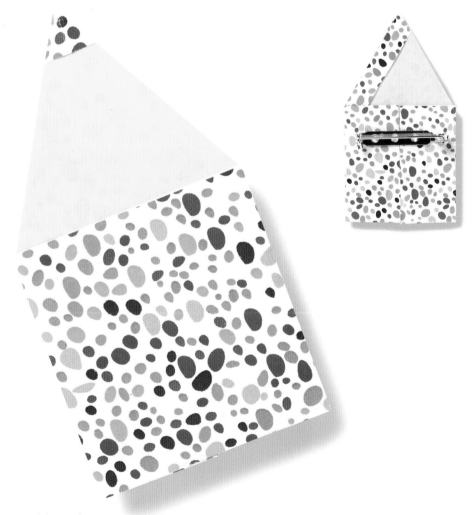

For recommended paper, see pp. 173 and 175
Cut two 8cm (3⅛in) squares as marked on reverse

1 **Fold** a strip backwards along the top edge of one of the squares

2 **Lightly mark** halfway and a quarter of the way from the right side

3 **Fold** the top left corner as shown, starting the fold from the middle

4 **Fold** the other side down over the folded left side

5 **Fold** the other square in half and open

6 **Place** the folded unit from step 4 on the centre fold of the folded square and fold up

7 **Fold in** the sides as shown and glue the flaps

Attach a brooch pin to the back

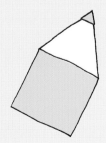

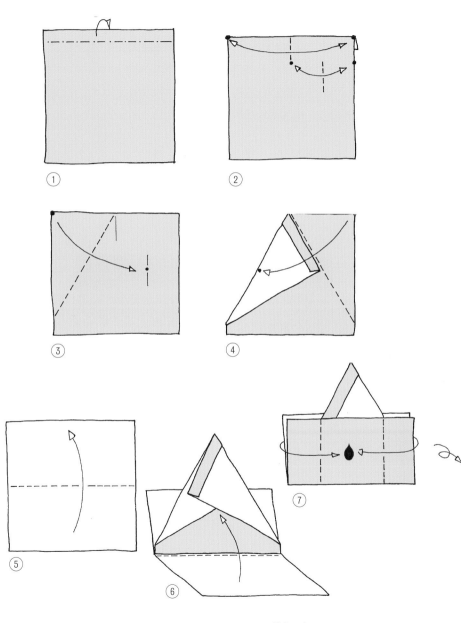

Kimono pin

This kimono-shaped brooch makes a stylish addition to your jewellery collection.

For recommended paper, see pp. 177 and 179
Cut a 10cm (4in) square as marked on reverse

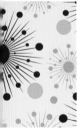

1 **Fold up** a strip of less than a third of the square

2 **Fold in** the right side at exactly a third of the way in

3 **Fold** the right side on the diagonal as shown. Then fold in the left side

4 **Fold** the left side on the diagonal as shown

5 **Open out** the sides

6 **Unfold** the strip at the base

7 **Fold in** the right side to join the dots, then fold up the strip again at the base

8 **Fold in** the sides, right side on top of the left

9 **Fold back** the top and side edgesas shown

To finish the brooch, glue a brooch pin to the back

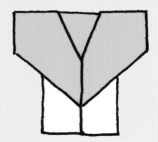

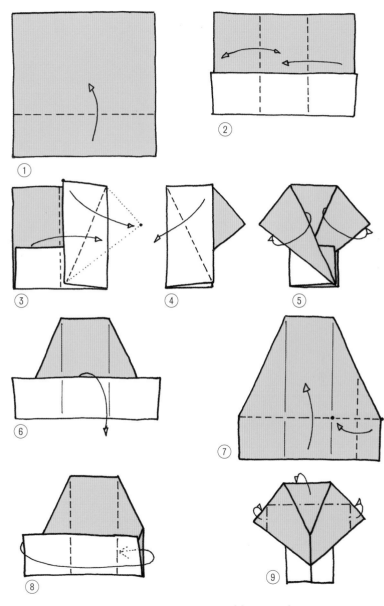

Kaleidoscope brooch

The Russian doll patterned paper makes a colourful brooch.

For recommended paper, see pp. 181 and 183
Cut two 8cm (3⅛in) squares as marked on reverse

1. **Mark** the middle of the lower edge and one diagonal, then fold in half along the other diagonal

2. **Fold up** the right tip to the dot marked to make a mark on the right-hand side

3. **Fold down** the triangles from this mark as shown, to the front and to the back

4. **Bend in** the left tip along the edge of the triangle without folding

5. **Fold in** the other side to the dot marked then unfold the two sides

6. **Bend** without folding to the dots marked then unfold and open

7. **Fold in** the two triangles then turn over

8. **Fold in** the corners as shown and then turn over. Repeat steps 1 to 7 to make the second part of the model

To assemble the brooch

9. **Place** the two parts one on top of the other, sliding the sides under the small squares

10. **Glue** the folds from behind and attach a brooch pin to the back

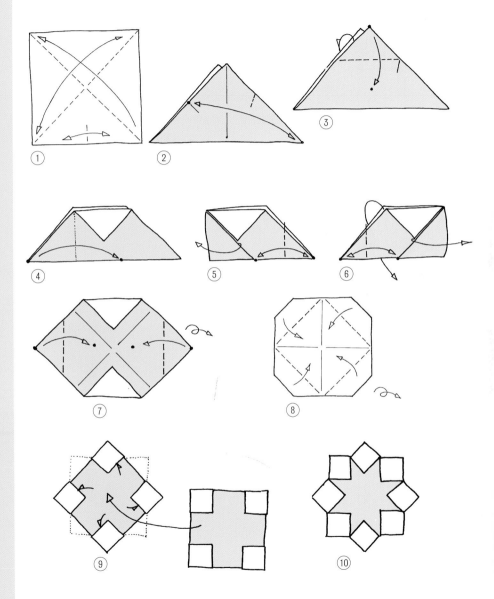

kaleidoscope brooch > 51

Calyx pin

The unusual shape of this simple and elegant brooch is inspired by the shape of flower petals.

For recommended paper, see pp. 185 and 187
Cut a 8cm (3⅛in) square as marked on reverse

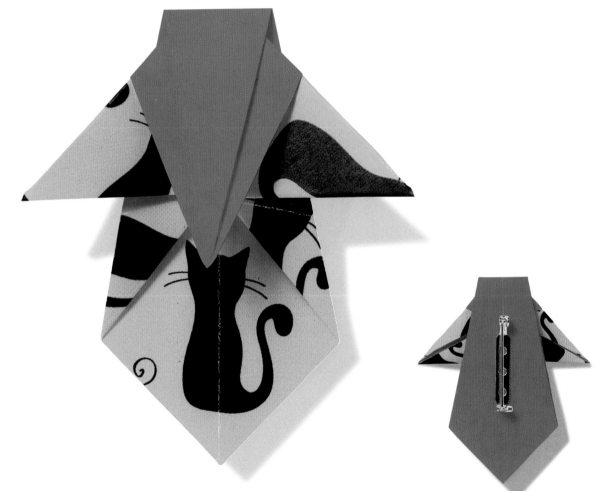

1. **Fold in** the sides to the centre fold

2. **Check** your model is as shown, then turn over

3. **Fold** the sides, releasing the back folds

4. **Bend** the top towards the bottom to join the dots and mark the fold. Fold up the left-hand side, in the same way as shown here with the right-hand side, which has the upper part folded to face the back

5. **Fold** the tip, and then fold the left-hand side as in the previous step, folding in the upper part

6. **Check** your model is as shown, then turn over

7. **Fold** the sides as shown to the left, checking your model is as shown on the right, then turn over

   To finish glue a brooch pin to the back

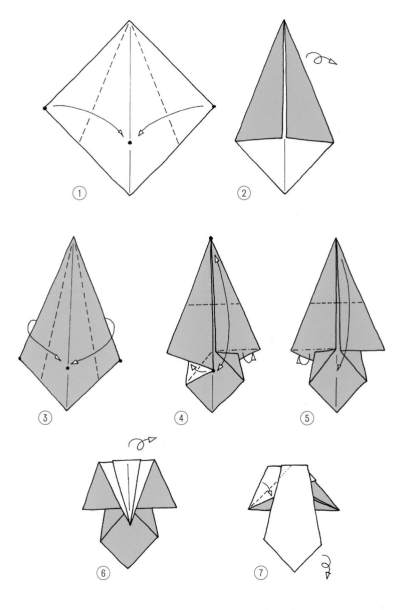

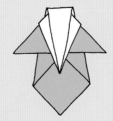

Chain bracelet

For recommended paper,
see pp. 189, 191, 193, 195, 197, 199 and 201
Cut eight 8cm (3⅛in) squares as marked on reverse

This colourful bracelet is made of individually folded units that slot together to form an interlocking chain.

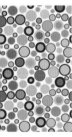

1 **Mark** the diagonal folds

2 **Fold** the corners into the centre

3 **Open out** the sides

4 **Fold** the sides in on themselves
   as shown

5 **Fold up** the top and bottom and mark
   the folds of the sides

6 **Make** an inside inverted fold (see p. 13)
   on both sides

7 **Fold** the corners back and glue

8 **Open out** the sides

9 **Repeat** steps 1 to 8 to make as many
   units as necessary (this will vary
   depending on the size of your wrist but
   seven or eight should be sufficient). To
   make the bracelet, slide the pieces into
   each other and glue in place

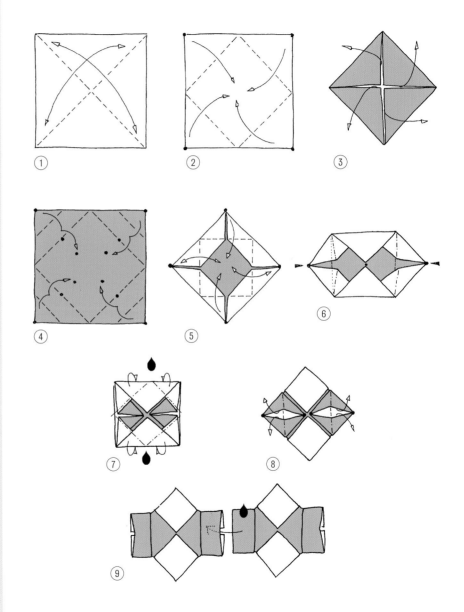

Boxes and decorations

Photo frame

An easy-to-make frame for displaying all your favourite photographs.

For recommended paper, see pp. 203 and 205

1 **Cut** the paper square in half for folding units A and B.

2 **Mark** the folds by folding in the sides to the centre

3 **Fold in** the sides along the fold lines shown

4 **Mark** the corner folds (B only)

5 **Invert** the corner folds then fold in the sides (B only)

To assemble the photo frame

6 **Place** unit B on top of unit A

7 **Fold in** the sides of unit A slotting them under the folded corners of unit B to finish the frame

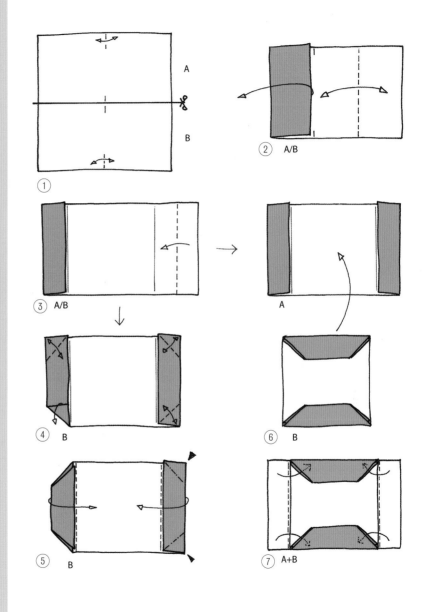

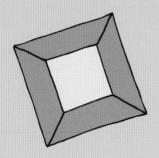

Crooked picture

This unusual frame focuses the eye on the subject of the picture, and it is ideal for displaying a portrait photo or a specialist picture such as Linda-Laure Greff's Kokeshi doll prints.

For recommended paper, see p. 207

1. **Cut** the sheet in half

2. **Mark** the folds on each half sheet, folding in the sides to the centre

3. **Fold** the top right and bottom left corners into triangles and then fold the left side along the diagonal as shown

4. **Repeat** this fold on the right-hand side, as shown

5. **Repeat** steps 3 and 4 for the second piece of paper, then place one sheet on top of the other as shown

6. **Fold in** the sides, slotting them inside each other

   The frame is complete

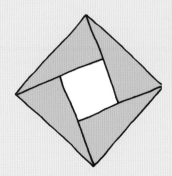

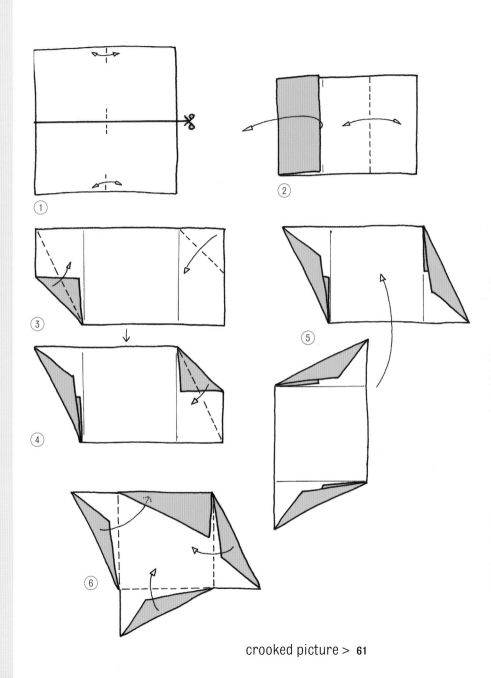

Swirling star

Attached to a wire, this star transforms into a celestial body, spinning infinitely in multicoloured swirls.

For recommended paper, see pp. 209, 211 and 213
Use two sheets of paper each cut into four squares

1 **Place** four cut squares together, two of each colour as shown. Mark the middle edge of one side of each square and then fold each side to the fold lines shown

2 **Fold** the sides to the centre as shown

3 **Check** your model is as shown, then turn over

4 **Fold** one tip towards the centre

5 **Then** the second

6 **Then** the third

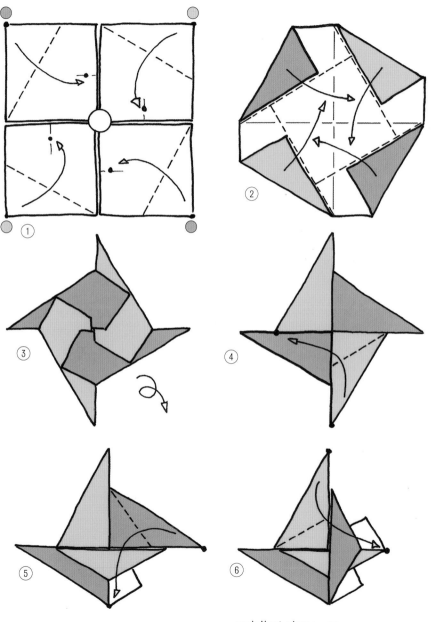

7 **Then fold** the last one in and under

8 **Fold** the four tips as before

9 **Finally**, fold each tip, one on top of the other. Cut the end of the last tip to help close the centre

10 **Fold in** the white part from below as shown

11 **Make** a double-sided star by putting two stars back to back as shown

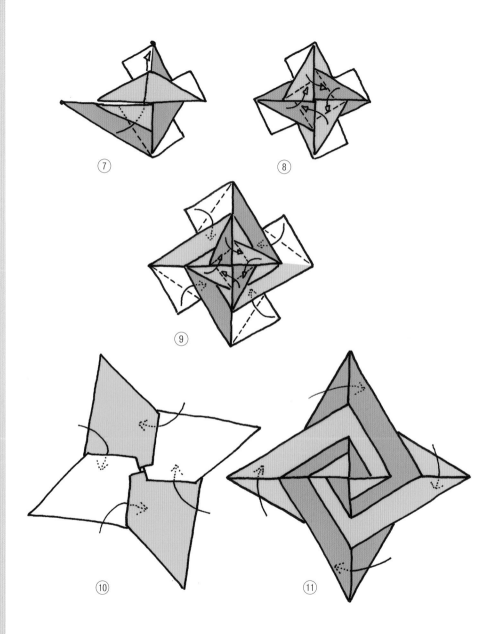

Bird ornament

You can either hang up this flying bird decoration, or display it in front of a mirror for an all-round view of its beautiful plumage.

For recommended paper, see pp. 215 and 217

Cut half a sheet diagonally

1 **Cut** the square in half along the diagonal

2 **Fold** the tips to the centre. Mark the fold on the left-hand side

3 **Fold up** the left tip along the fold line shown and then mark the fold on the right-hand side

4 **Fold up** the right-hand tip and then turn over

5 **Fold up** the central triangle

6 **Mark** the centre fold of the two tips

7 **Fold up** the two tips then turn the whole thing over

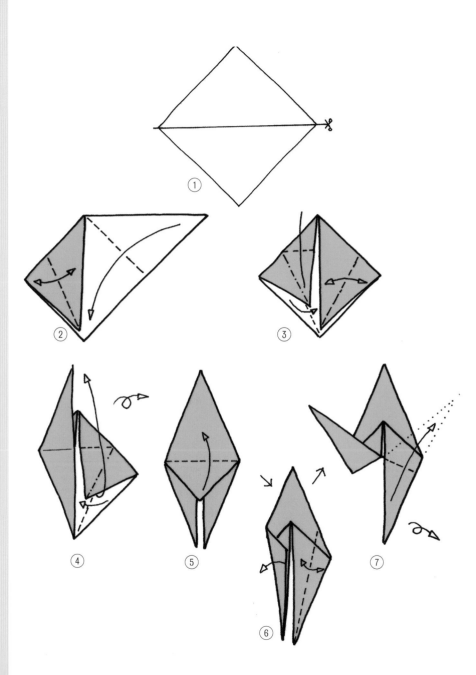

8 **Fold** the tips in half along the fold lines shown

9 **Make** an outside inverted fold on one of the tips (see p. 13) to form the head then fold down the central part

9a **Close up** of the head

10 **Place** the bird on a mirror to see it in full

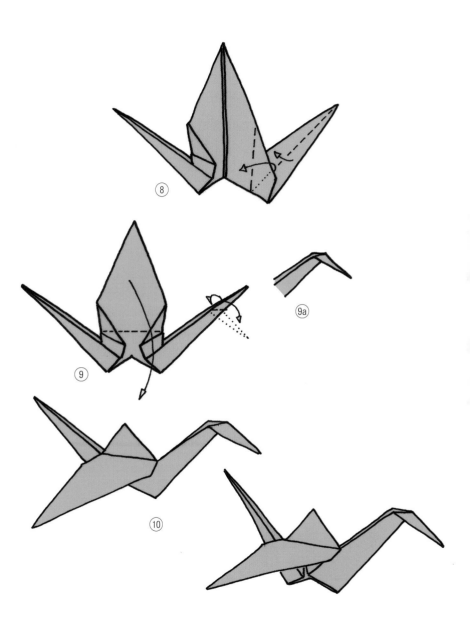

Kimono chain

Add a Japanese touch to your home with this delightful garland featuring little paper chain men dressed in kimonos.

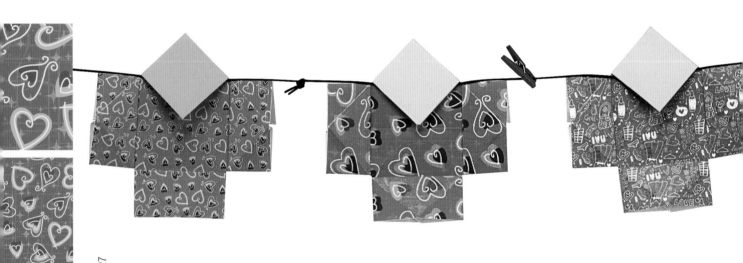

For recommended paper,
see pp. 219, 221, 223, 225 and 227

1. **Mark** the folds as indicated

2. **Fold** the corners to the centre, then unfold the bottom two

3. **Check** your model is as shown, then turn over

4. **Roll** the top corners inwards, folding as shown

5. **Fold** the side and bottom corners to the centre, joining the dots, then unfold the sides

6. **Make** inside inverted folds (see p. 13) at each side

7. **Fold down** the upper tip as shown

8. **Fold back** the four corners

9. **Open** the sides and the bottom as shown to complete the kimono shape

Make several and thread or clip onto a cord to make the garland

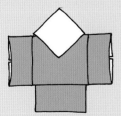

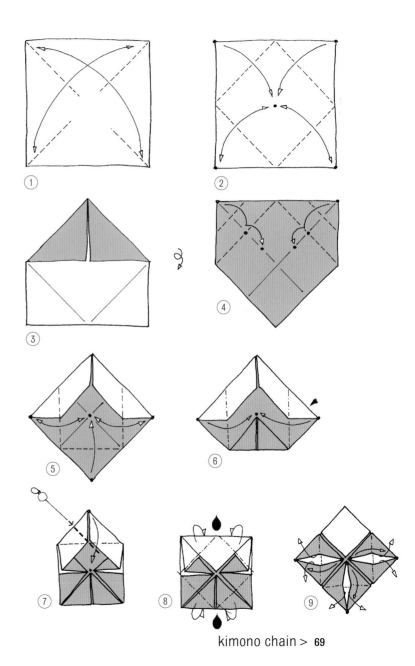

Blooming flowers

Two pretty flowers that, with a quick press of the fingers, will bloom in your hands.

For recommended paper, see pp. 229, 231 and 233

1. **Make** a diamond base (see p. 15) then mark the folds, joining the dots

2. **Unfold**

3. **Fold up** the two sides at the same time

   Details

4. **Turn** the first section

5. **Slide** it inside, adding a dab of glue

6. **Turn** the other section

7. **Slide** it inside as before

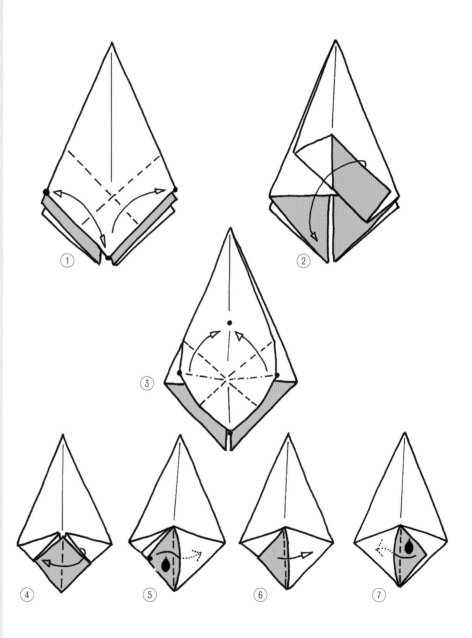

8 Rotate the unit to fold the other three
faces in the same way (steps 1 to 7)

9 Cut the top as shown and then press
the lower part to fully open the flower
(see step 10)

9a Cut in this alternative way for a
different shaped flower

10 Open up the flower

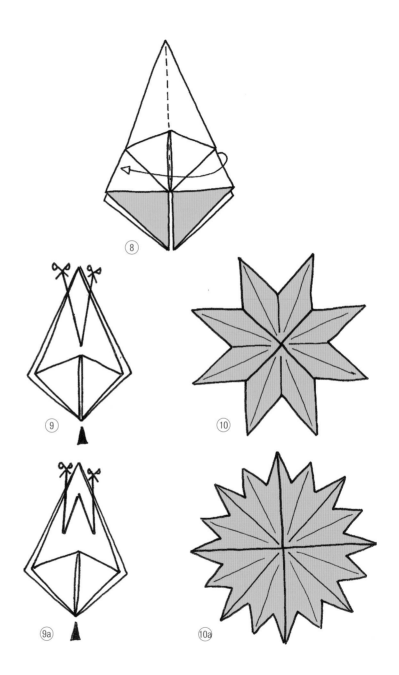

Variation

1 **Cut** a pentagon (5 sides) and then fold as shown

2 **Mark** the folds, folding in the sides to the centre

3 **Lift** the flap vertically, then open out and flatten

4 **Repeat** steps 2 and 3 for the other four faces

5 **Turn over** one petal

6 **Mark** the folds

7 **Unfold** and then repeat steps 1 to 8 on pages 71–72

8 **Cut** the top in a rounded shape as shown and then press the lower part to fully open the flower

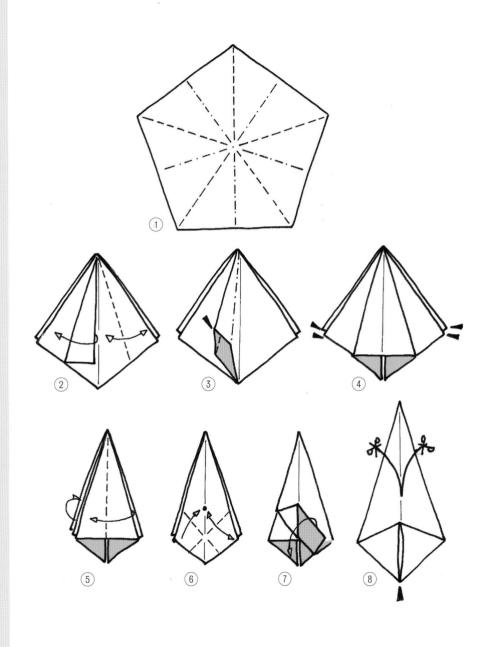

Scented bottles

To make a simple air freshener to brighten up any room, just add a drop of perfume onto these small bottles so that they give off a subtle fragrance.

For recommended paper, see pp. 235, 237, 239 and 241

Cut half a sheet of paper per bottle as marked on reverse

1 **Cut** a square in half

2 **Fold in** the sides to the centre

3 **Mark** a fold a third of the way down

4 **Mark** the top part a third of the way in on either side, then fold down

5 **Fold** the corners to mark the folds

Details

6 **Roll** a strip of around 5mm (¼in)

7 **Mark** a final mountain fold (see p. 12) (**1**), then unfold partially (**2**)

8 **Fold again**

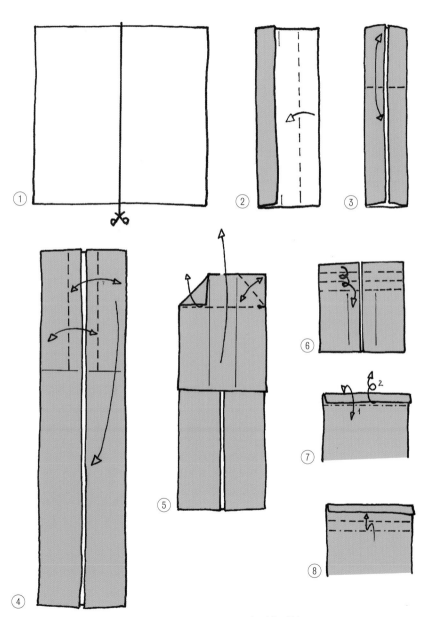

9 **Fold** the left side, pushing down to form the triangle marked

10 **Lift** the top edge before folding the right side in the same way

11 **Slot in** the upper edge of the cork, then refold, joining the dots

12 **Fold down** the top corners, mark the side folds and then open out

13 **Fold** the sides in and the base up, tucking under the side corners as you do so, then turn over

14 **The bottle** is complete

Adapt the design to make a different shaped bottle

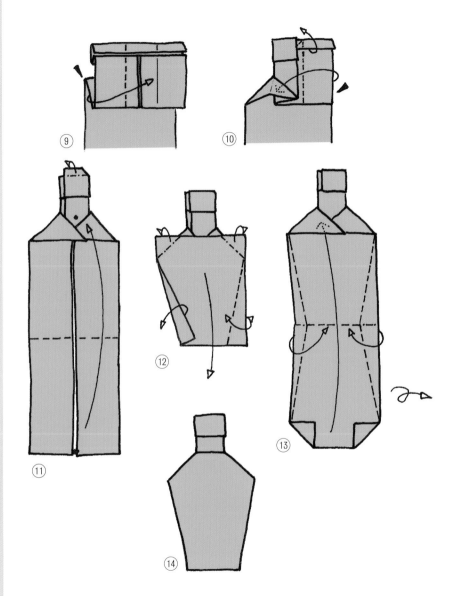

Gift box

For this lovely little gift box the base and the lid are folded in exactly the same way using different papers for each.

For recommended paper, see pp. 243, 245, 247 and 249
Use two sheets of paper

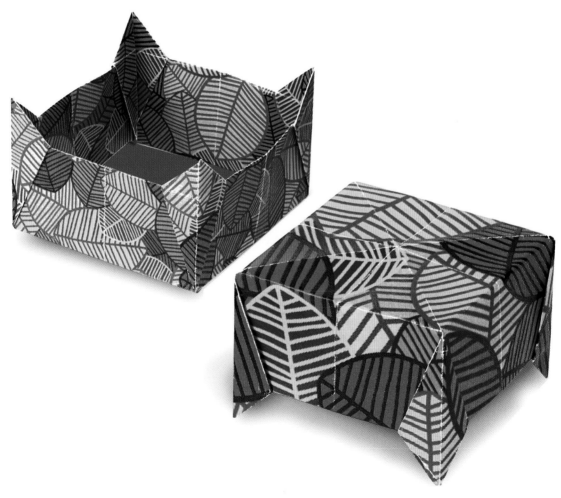

1. **Mark** the folds, turning in the corners to the centre

2. **Fold in** the four corners as shown, then fold along the fold marks shown to form a preliminary base (see p. 14)

3. **Fold** the four sides as shown, then mark the folds of the left-hand triangle one by one

3a. **Lift** the triangle vertically, then open out and flatten. Repeat on the other three sides

4. **Fold in** the upper part on both sides and then turn two of the sections, one to the front, one to the back

5. **Fold in** the last two sides and then mark the fold for the base of the box before pushing it into shape by pressing on the point at the base

6. **Make the cover** in the same way and place on the box base between the four tips

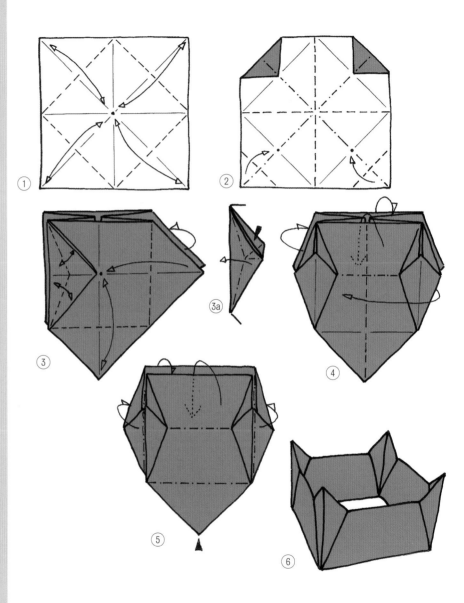

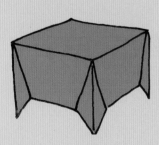

Bead tray

This double-sided unit, which can be slotted onto a base tube to make a multi-compartment storage tray, is ideal for keeping beads or other small craft materials separate as you work.

For recommended paper, see pp. 251, 253 and 255
Cut half a sheet and a rectangle 8 x 19.5cm (3⅛ x 7⅝in)
as marked on reverse

To make a bead tray

1 **Cut** the square in half

2 **Mark** the folds as shown

3 **Fold** the top and bottom edges to the centre fold

4 **Mark** the folds, folding in the sides to the centre, then turn over

5 **Lift** the top and bottom edges and then mark the triangle folds

6 **Fold** back each of the four sides to make these triangles appear

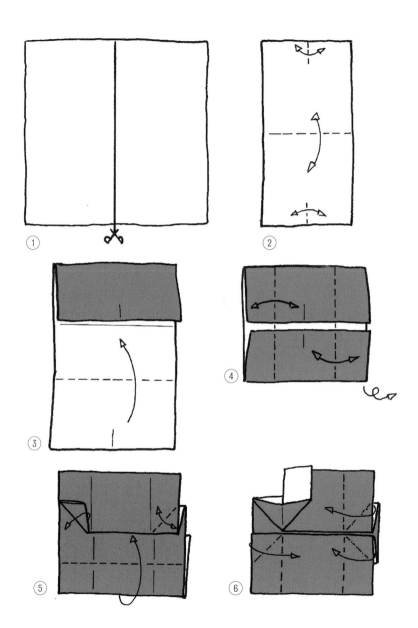

7 **Check** your model is as shown, then turn over

8 **Fold** the sides to the centre

9 **Mark** the folds as shown, then slot the ends together to complete the tray

To make the base tube

10 **Cut** an 8 x 19.5cm rectangle (3⅛ x 7⅝in) from the remaining half of paper, then fold in four and roll into a triangle

11 **Check** our model is as shown

12 **The base tube** is complete; slot on several tray units along the tube

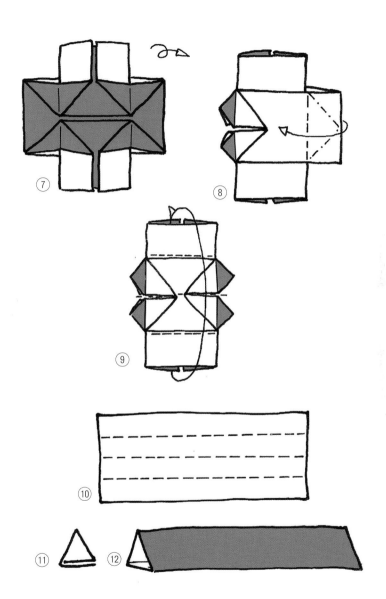

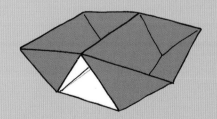

Trinket tray

This elegant trinket tray is ideal for storing all your small treasures.

For recommended paper, see pp. 257 and 259

1 **Fold** the corners to the centre along the fold marks shown

2 **Make** a waterbomb base (see p. 14)

3 **Fold up** the four tips in the same way, then unfold completely

4 **Fold** the four corners underneath, then fold the centre part (**1**) before folding back the edges along the folds (**2**) as shown. Repeat on all sides

5 **Push** the trinket tray into shape by folding the four flaps under. Turn over

6 **Re-mark** all the folds to finish the tray

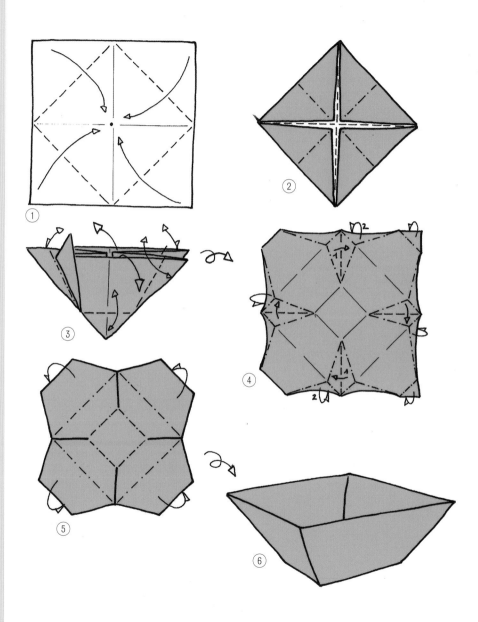

Little dish

Keep this little dish on your bedside table – it makes the perfect place to store all the bits and pieces that accumulate in your pockets throughout the day.

For recommended paper, see pp. 261, 263 and 265

1 **Mark** the folds, folding the corners to the centre

2 **Fold** the triangles in on themselves as shown

3 **Fold** along the fold lines shown

4 **Fold** the four tips, mark the lower triangle, then unfold and turn over

5 **Fold** into shape as shown

Details for shaping

6 **Fold** joining the dots

7 **Fold** joining the dots

8 **Fold** the surplus part underneath. Repeat on all sides

The trinket dish is complete

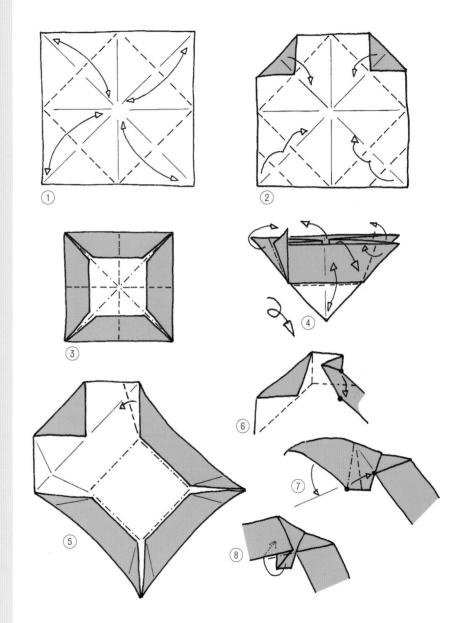

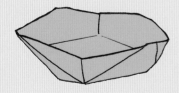

Eight-petal flower

Eight small squares are all you need to make this flower – one for each of the petals.

For recommended paper, see pp. 267, 269, 271 and 273
Use two sheets each cut into four 8cm (3⅛in) squares as marked on reverse

To make the petals

1 **Fold** the sides of each square along the centre fold

2 **Fold up** the tip, joining the dots (**1**), then unfold (**2**)

3 **Fold up** along the fold line shown

4 **Fold** the sides in (**1**), then fold the bottom tip down (**2**)

5 **Fold in** the sides, then turn over

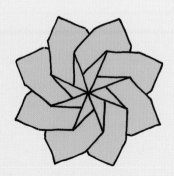

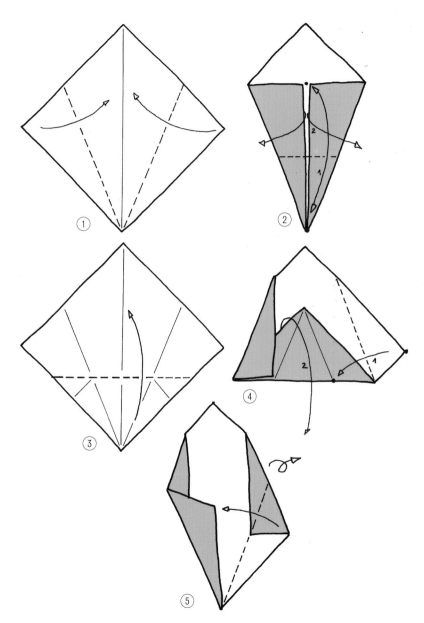

eight-petal flower > **87**

6 **Fold up** the bottom tip along the fold line shown. Make eight petals in all

To assemble the petals

7 **Check** your model is as shown. The central part will enable you to attach each petal to the left and to the right. Slot the corner of one petal into the central part of the petal to the left, then gently turn the petal from above to the left

8 **Slot** the other corner in the same way into the right and then turn over

9 **Slot** the corner underneath

10 **Repeat** steps 8 and 9 to assemble the other petals

11 **The flower** is complete

12 **Turn over** for the back view

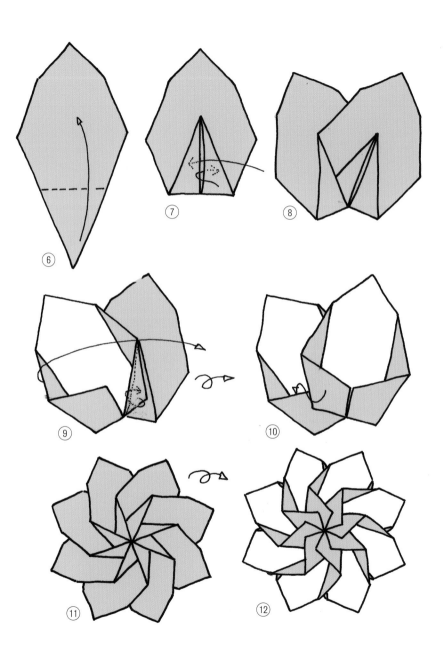

Animal mobile

Strings of teddy bear and puppy dog faces make a colourful decoration for a child's room.

For recommended paper, see pp. 275, 277, 279, 281, 283, 285, 287, 289 and 291
Use one sheet of paper cut into four 8cm (3⅛in) squares to make four heads

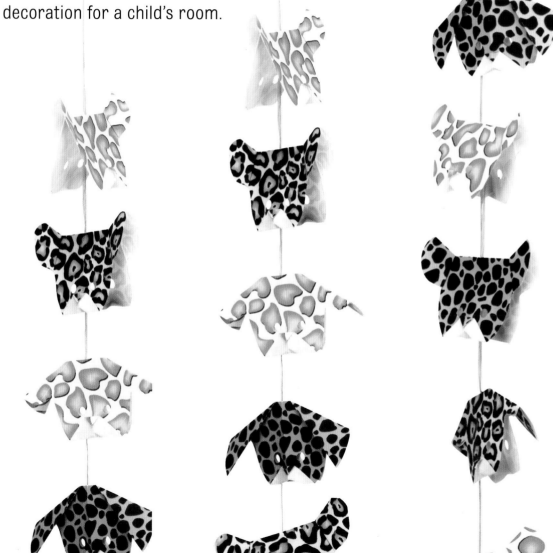

To make the teddy bear face

1 **Fold** a small square in half

2 **Fold** in half from side to side

3 **Cut** along the solid lines shown and make a hole for the eyes, then fold the ears

4 **Unfold** the ears, then unfold the whole thing

5 **Fold** the ears as shown first, then fold the whole thing in half

6 **Check** your model is as shown. Fold up the bottom to the front and on the reverse

7 **Fold** a triangle at the front tip to make the nose

Shape the base of the teddy bear's face to complete

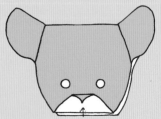

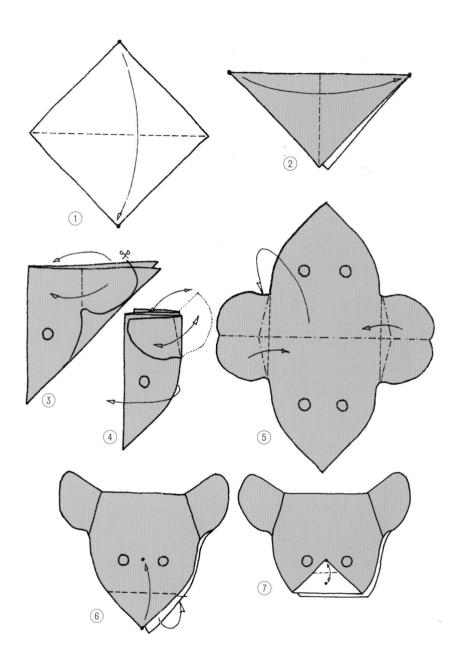

To make the puppy dog face

1 **Repeat** steps 1 and 2 of the teddy
   bear face, then cut along the sold lines
   shown. Make a hole for the eyes, then
   unfold as shown

2 **Check** your model is as shown. Now
   fold down the two ears, then fold up the
   bottom to the front and the reverse

3 **Fold** a triangle at the front tip to make
   the nose

4 **Shape** the base of the puppy dog's face
   to complete

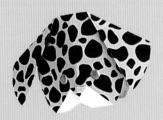

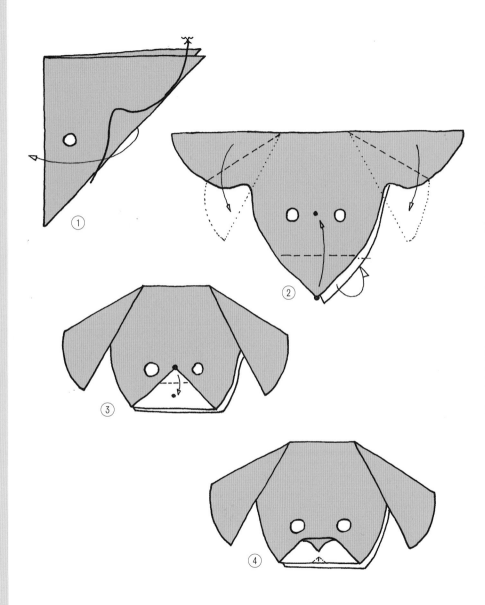

Gifts and messages

Pencil pot

This box is designed to store colouring pencils or pens and its wooden handle makes it very portable.

1. **Mark** the folds as shown

2. **Fold** the two vertical sides a quarter of the way in

3. **Fold** along the fold lines shown

4. **Fold** the four sides along the centre fold

5. **Fold** the sides to the centre, then fold the tab on the left, slotting it inside the folds of the triangle

6. **Repeat** with the other three tabs. Make two holes for the handle, then mark the base and press the tip to push the box into shape

7. **Slide** a stick or a small pencil handle through the holes at the top of the box

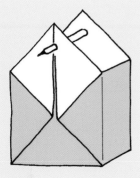

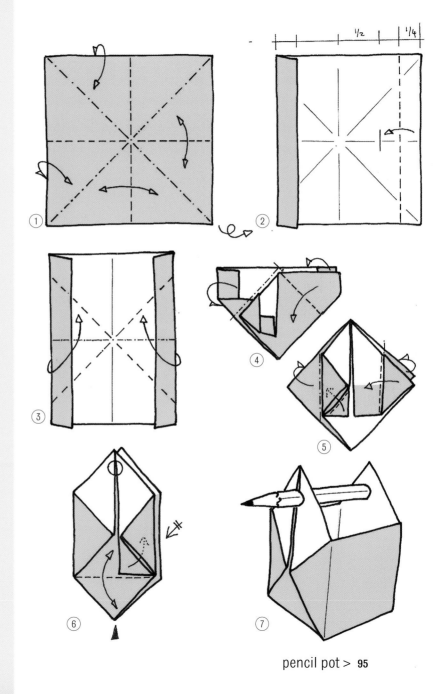

Pencil bookmark

A strip of paper can easily be transformed into this pencil-shaped bookmark. Make several to give to your friends.

For recommended paper, see pp. 297, 299 and 301

Cut a 4cm (1½in) wide strip for each bookmark as marked on reverse

1 **Fold** the short ends of the strip to the reverse by approximately 5mm (¼in)

2 **Fold** the top corner as shown

3 **Fold down** the top corners once again, as shown, then turn over

4 **Mark** the vertical folds a third of the way in

5 **Fold in half** to join the dots, then turn over

6 **Fold** in three, slotting the sides into each other. Turn over

The pencil is complete

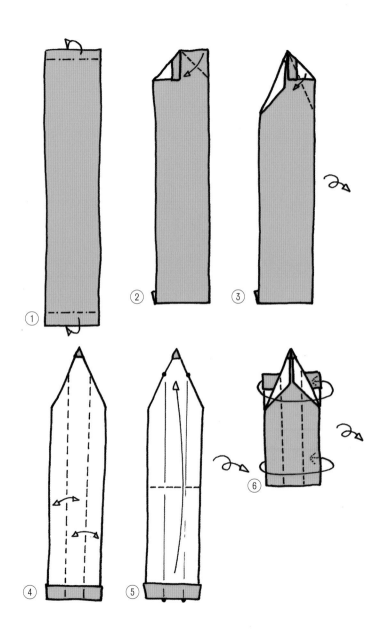

Secret box

Here's a box with an opening so discreet that all your secrets will be well hidden.

For recommended paper, see pp. 303 and 305
Use two sheets of paper

1 **Mark** the centre and then mark the first folds by folding the corners into the centre as shown. Fold the four small triangles in on themselves

2 **Check** your model is as shown, then turn over

3 **Fold** the sides into the centre

4 **Fold** the four corners under the uppermost part

5 **Open** out wide

6 **Keep** the bottom flat as you do so

7 **Make** another identical unit for the box lid

The secret box is complete

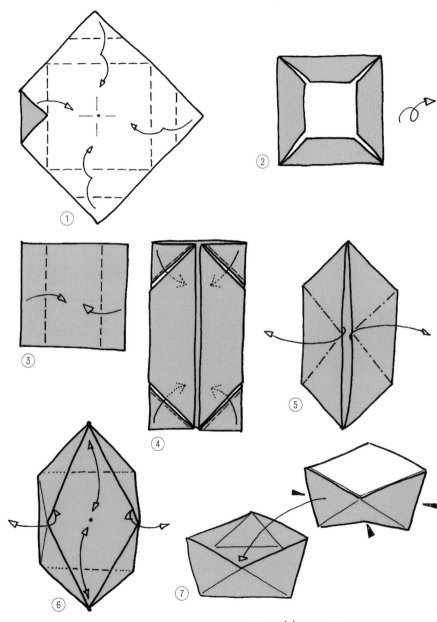

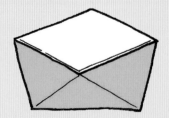

secret box > **99**

Flower pot

This paper pot makes a perfect vase for a bouquet of freshly-picked flowers.

For recommended paper, see pp. 307, 309, 311 and 313

1 **Fold** a strip a quarter of the way in at the top and bottom edges of the paper, then fold along the centre fold

2 **Fold** the sides up to the centre fold as shown

3 **Check** your model is as shown, then unfold

4 **Fold** to the right (**1**), opening the left side flat (**2**)

5 **Check** your model is as shown, then turn over

6 **Repeat** for the other side

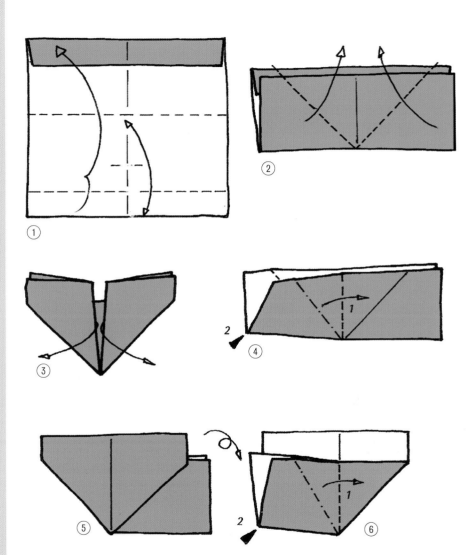

7 Fold in the sides to join the dots, back and front

8 Fold the sides again, back and front, to join the dots as shown

9 Fold the upper tip in two under the sides, then fold the centre tabs between the folded layers

10 Mark the bottom fold as shown, then press the point to push the flower pot into shape

11 The flower pot is complete

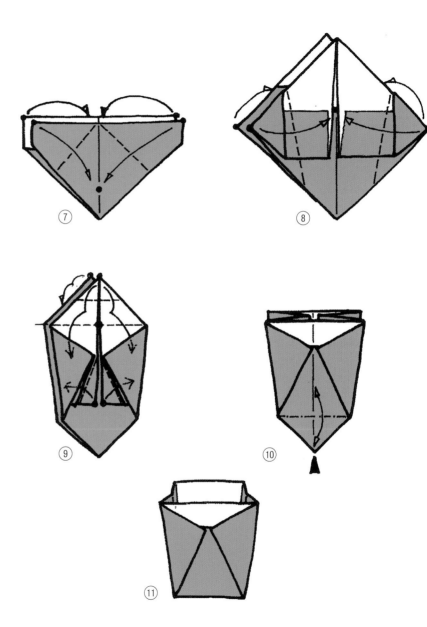

Change of heart bookmark

This small heart-shaped bookmark is magic. By simply turning the sides, a second heart is revealed.

For recommended paper, see pp. 315 and 317
Use half a sheet of paper as marked on reverse

1 **Cut** a square in half

2 **Fold** one of the rectangles in half horizontally

3 **Fold in** the sides along the centre fold, then turn over

4 **Flip** the whole thing forward by folding as shown

5 **Check yo**ur model is as shown, then unfold

6 **Fold** following the direction of the folds as shown

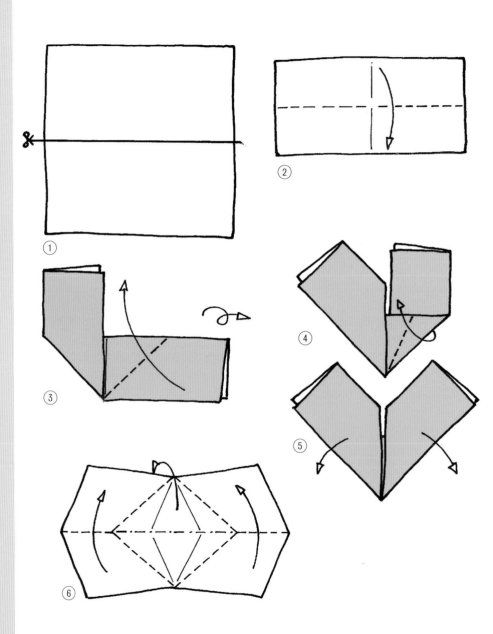

7. **Fold** down the top part as shown and then unfold

8. **Fold in** the left side

9. **Fold in** the other side and then make an inside inverted fold (see p. 13) with the top parts

10. **Slot** the left tip inside the folded layers, then repeat the folds on the right side

11. **Fold in** the tip as before

12. **Transform** the heart by pulling the sides down using both hands

13. **Continue** until a central diamond appears. Once folded in half, another similar heart will appear

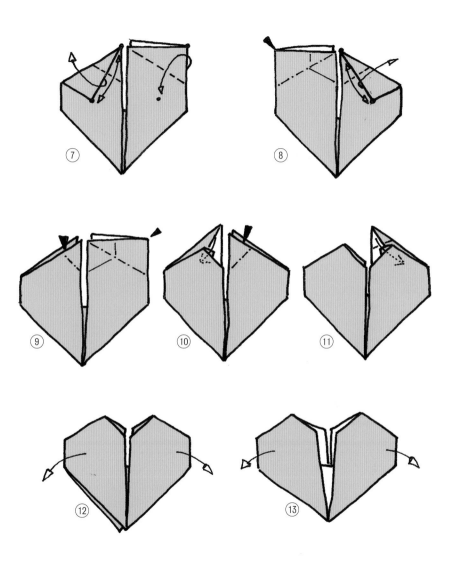

Heart-shaped gift box

This little heart-shaped box is ideal for presenting small jewellery gifts – simply place your love token inside its folds.

For recommended paper, see pp. 319 and 321

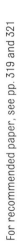

1. **Fold** the top and bottom edges of the paper a quarter of the way in

2. **Fold** in half

3. **Fold in** the sides to the centre fold, then turn over

4. **Flip** the whole thing forward by folding as shown, then unfold

5. **Refold** flat as shown

6. **Fold down** the flaps from the central edge, then fold the triangle on the left

7. **Fold in** the remaining flap on the right, then mark the fold by folding the left tip. Finally, fold the other right triangle

8. **Make** an inside inverted fold (see p. 13) to fold in the triangle (**1**) which is held in by the flap that is folded to the inside (**2**). Unfold the right side and repeat the folds from the previous step

9. **Fold in** the two tips with an inside inverted fold (see p. 13)

10. **To shape** the heart, put a surprise inside it, or simply pop a toothpick in to help it keep its shape

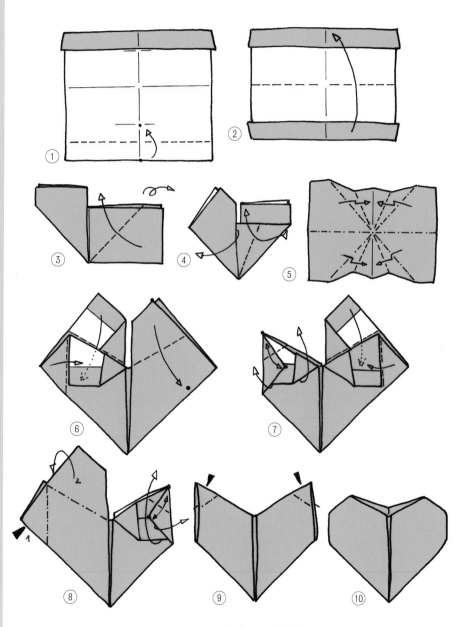

heart-shaped gift box > **107**

Love letters

Write your loving message on the inside of the square, before folding it up.

For recommended paper, see pp. 323 and 325

1 **Fold** the sides into the centre

2 **Fold in** the top corners

3 **Fold up** the base to join the dots, then unfold completely

4 **Fold** the bottom part as shown

5 **Fold in** the two bottom corners, then invert the left corner

6 **Fold over** the left side, then invert the right corner

7 **Fold in** the right side, then fold over the top left corner

8 **Fold over** the top right corner to complete the flaps

9 **Slide** the flap tip into the triangle slot beneath

The love letter is complete

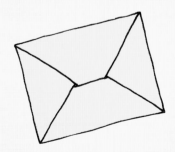

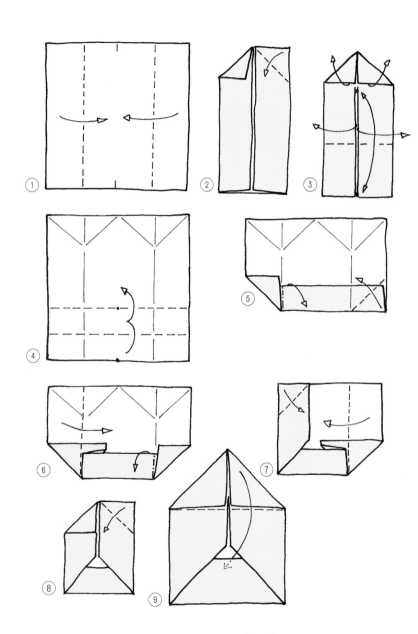

Envelope

Here's a folding envelope worth learning by heart for sending loving notes.

For recommended paper, see p. 327

1. **Fold up** the bottom tip to join the dots

2. **Fold down** the bottom tip to the bottom edge to join the dots

3. **Fold up** the bottom tip once more, and fold in the sides to mark the folds

4. **Slide** the central part behind by folding, then fold the two sides leaving 2mm (³⁄₃₂in). Finally, lift the centre part on the left

5. **Repeat** on the right and then lift the centre part once again. Fold the two sides as shown

6. **Fold down** the top flap to slot inside

The envelope is complete

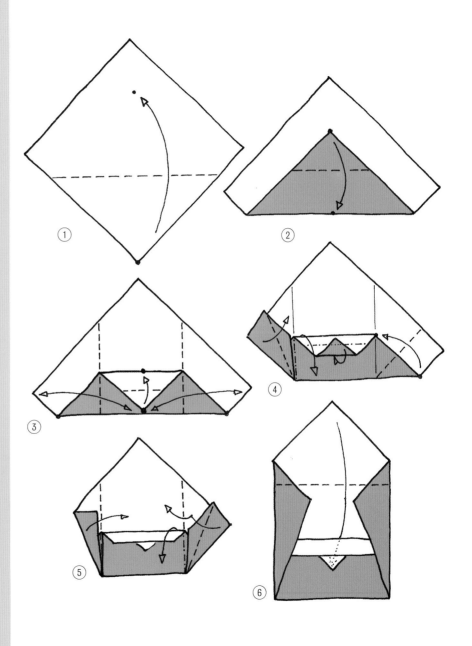

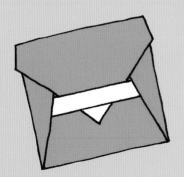

Hidden message

To discover your message, you simply have to gently unfold the sides without tearing.

For recommended paper, see pp. 329, 331 and 333
Cut paper into triangles as marked on reverse

1 **Fold** the triangle to join the dots

2 **Fold up** the tip in line with the central point

3 **Fold up** the left tip to join the dots

4 **Fold** the tip out, as in step 2

5 **Fold up** the right tip

6 **Fold** the tip out as before

7 **Overlap** the triangles

8 **Check** your model is as shown

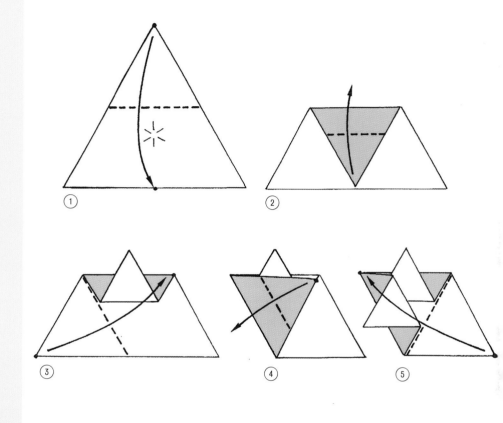

Variation 1

9a   **Fold** each triangle in half

10a **Mark** the folds to the centre

11a **Open** each tip

12a **Cross** the tips at the centre along the fold lines

13a **Fold** in the same way to complete the crossed legs variation

Variation 2

9b   **Fold** each triangle in half

10b **Fold** the overhang behind

11b **Check** your model is as shown for the finished triangle variation

Variation 3

9b   **Fold** each triangle in half

12b **Fold** the tips behind

13b **Check** your model is as shown for the finished hexagon variation

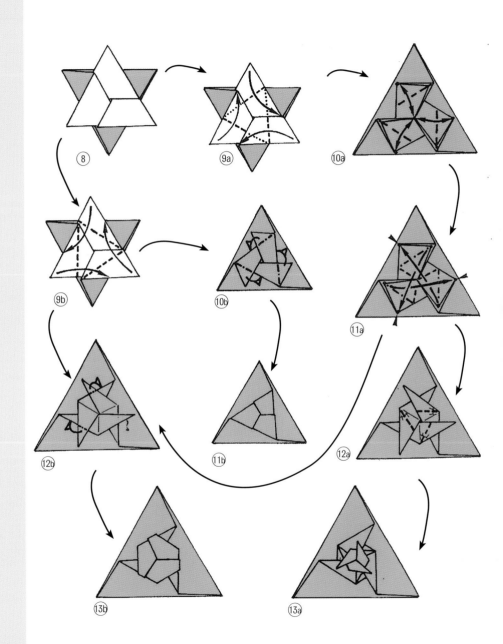

Jewellery box

This beautiful jewellery box is just the place for a small accessory.

For recommended paper, see pp. 335, 337 and 339

1 **Mark** the middle of the top edge and make a mark a quarter of the way in from the edge on the left-hand side of the square. Then starting from the first mark, fold down the top left corner to join the dot on the quarter way mark

2 **Fold down** the other corner

3 **Fold up** the strip at the base

4 **Fold down** the tip to join the dots at the middle of the bottom edge

5 **Mark** the folds in line with the triangle and then unfold completely

6 **Cut** along the solid lines then turn over one of the two pieces

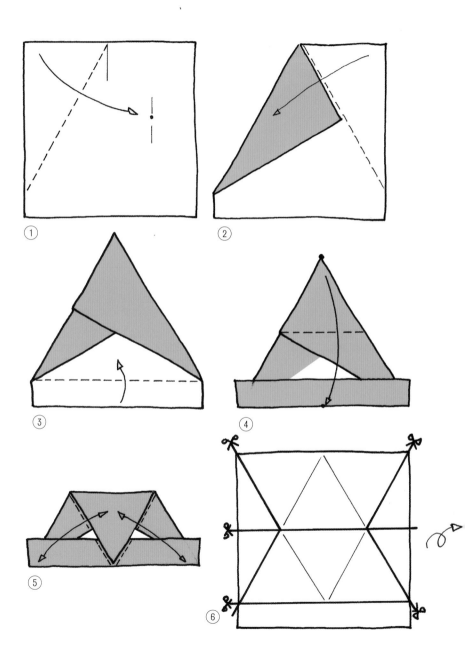

7 **Refold** the triangles as shown

8 **Mark** the fold on all layers by folding the tip to the middle of the opposite side

9 **Repeat** for the other two tips

10 **Fold** the tips to the centre, as shown

11 **Slot** the tips inside

12 **The jewellery box** is complete

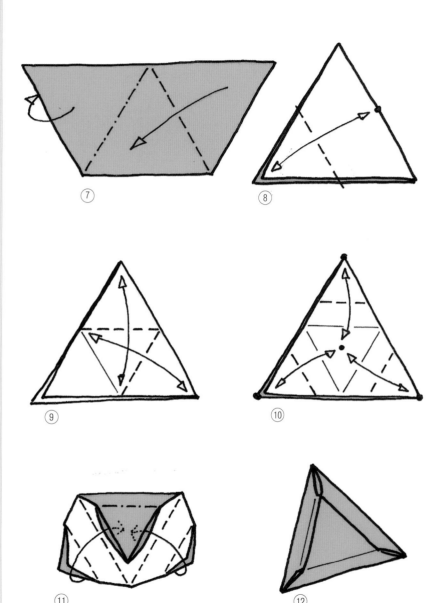

Clutch bag

A practical clutch bag for storing business cards and shopping receipts.

For recommended paper, see pp. 341 and 343

1 **Mark** the folds a quarter of the way in from the left and right edges of the paper and unfold (**1**). Fold up the bottom edge a third of the way up (**2**)

2 **Mark** a fold of approximately 5mm (¼in) at the bottom edge, then turn over

3 **Fold** the bottom corners to join the dots

4 **Open** the triangle slightly to fold the left flap along the fold mark. Do the same on the right side and then turn over

5 **Mark** the fold as shown, then turn over and unfold completely

6 **Mark** the vertical folds and you are now ready to put it together along the folds

7 **Fold** the corners on the top part as shown, and fold the bottom strip inwards on the bottom part

8 **Fold in** the top edges, blocking the inverted corner folds (**1**), and then fold the flap with two spaced out folds (**2**).

The clutch bag is complete

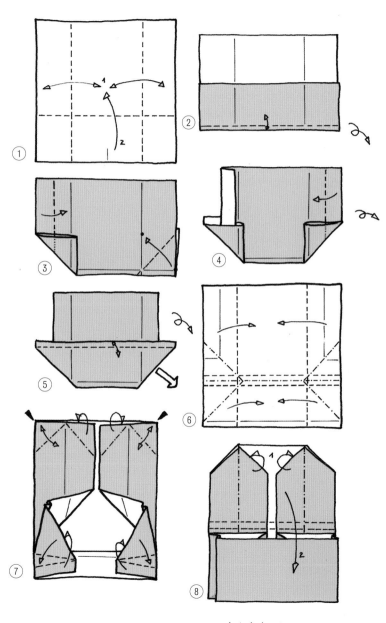

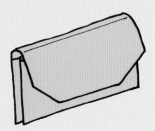

Paper

On the following pages you will find the various papers that were used to make the origami shown in this book. There are also stickers available so you can let you imagination run wild and add character to your origami model.

Recommended paper for Love charm: see diagrams and instructions on pp. 18–19

Recommended paper for Twirling leaves: see diagrams and instructions on pp. 20–21

Recommended paper for Twirling leaves: see diagrams and instructions on pp. 20–21

Recommended paper for Little fishes: see diagrams and instructions on pp. 24–25

Recommended paper for Little fishes: see diagrams and instructions on pp. 24–25

Recommended paper for Psychedelic hoops: see diagrams and instructions on pp. 26–27

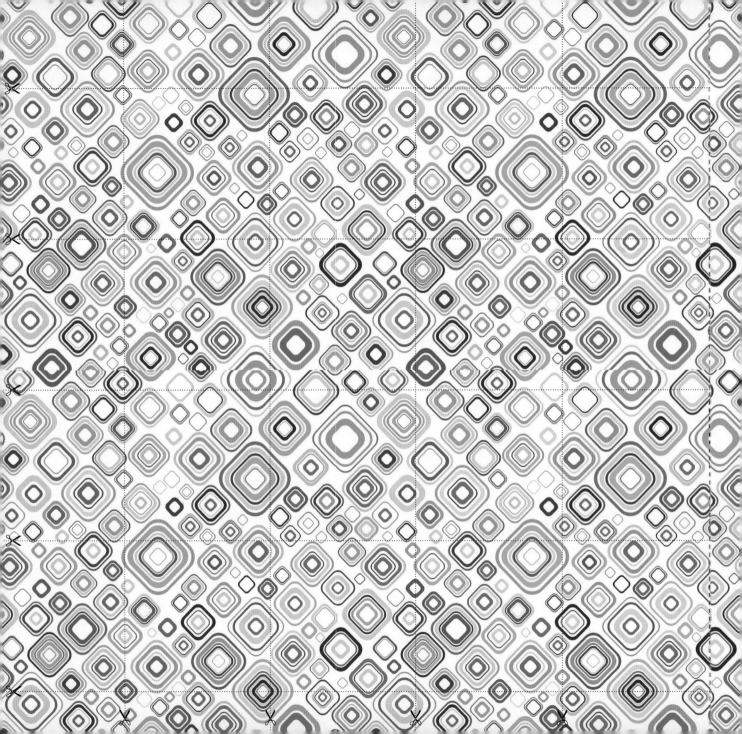

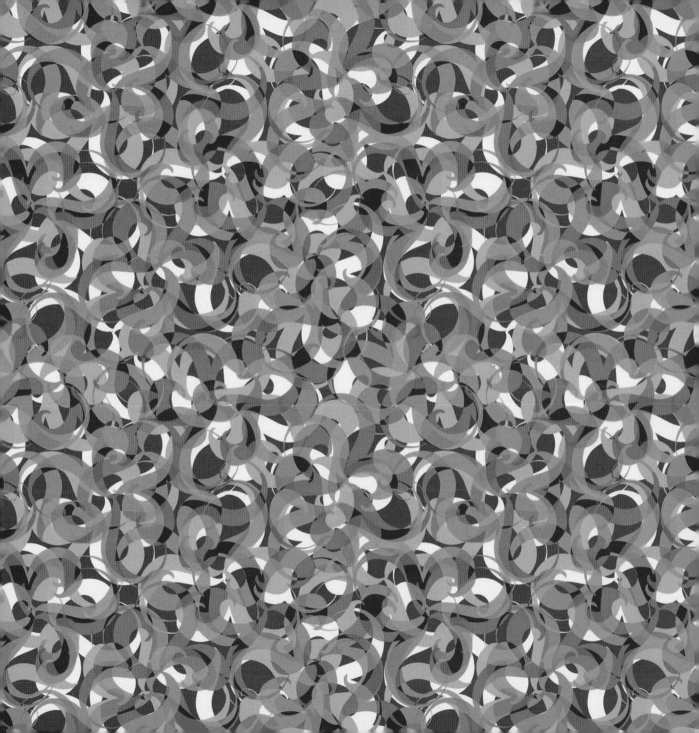

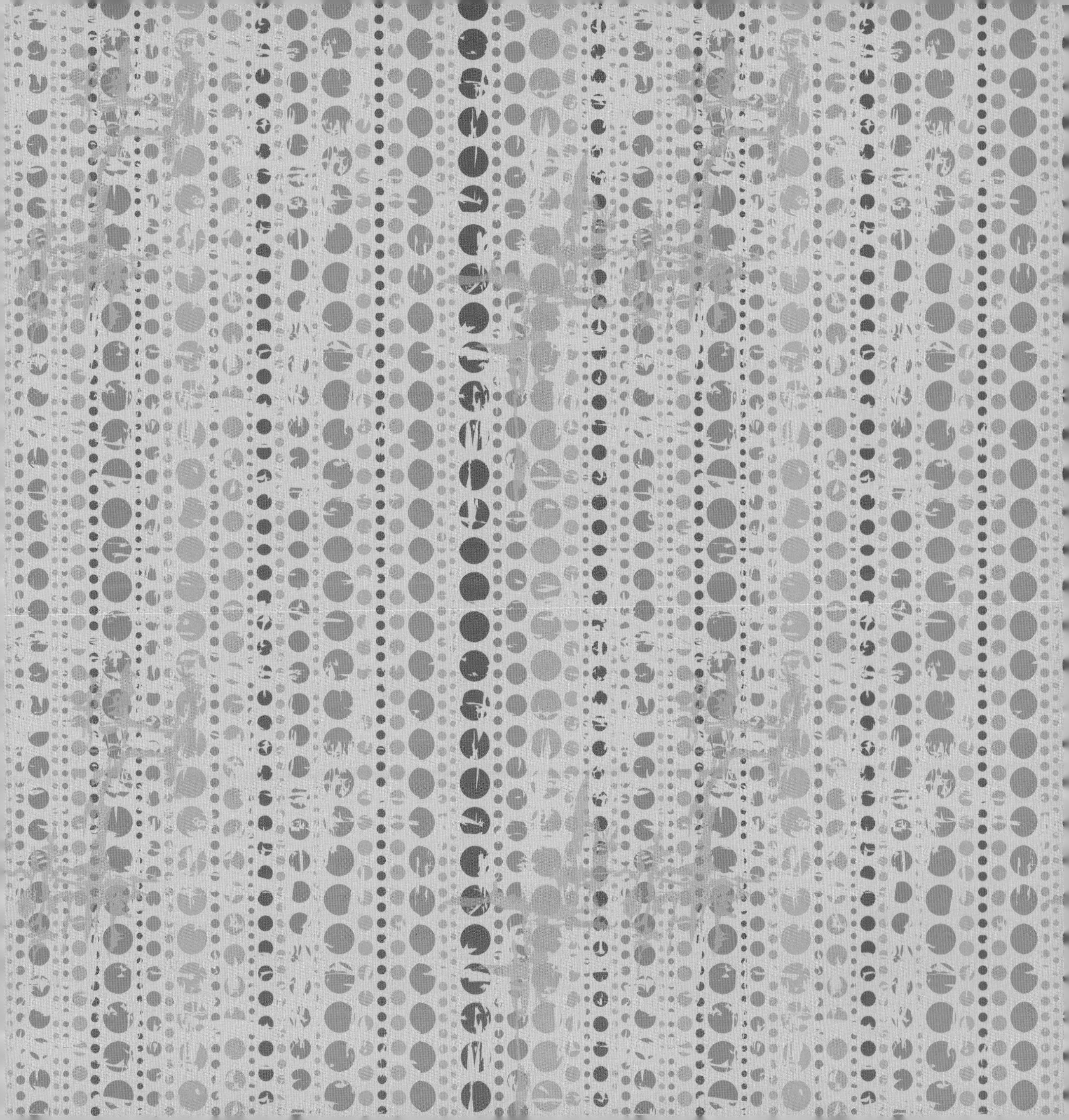

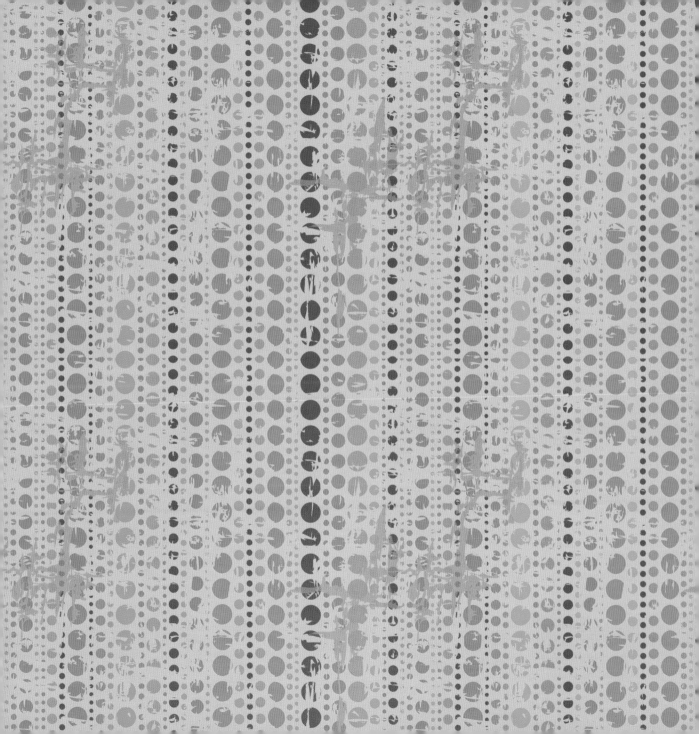

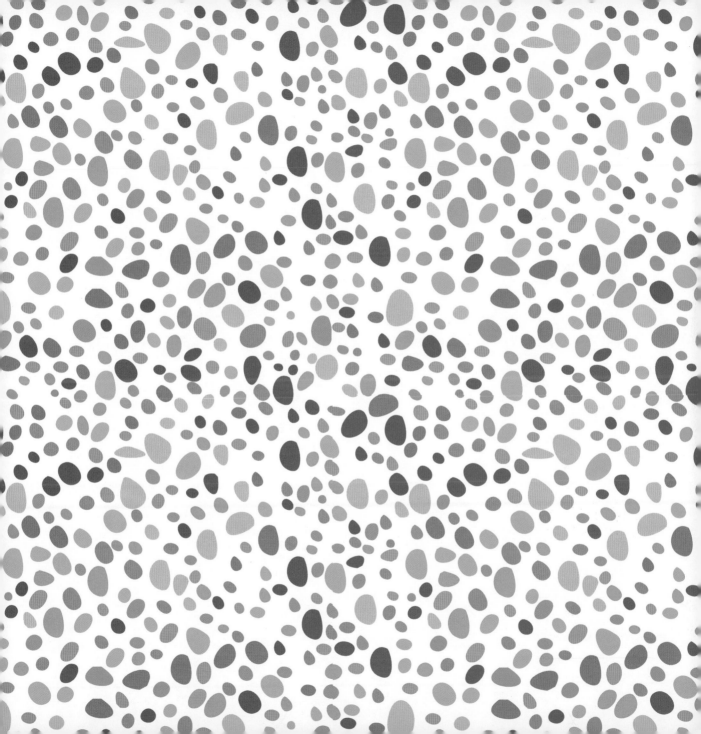

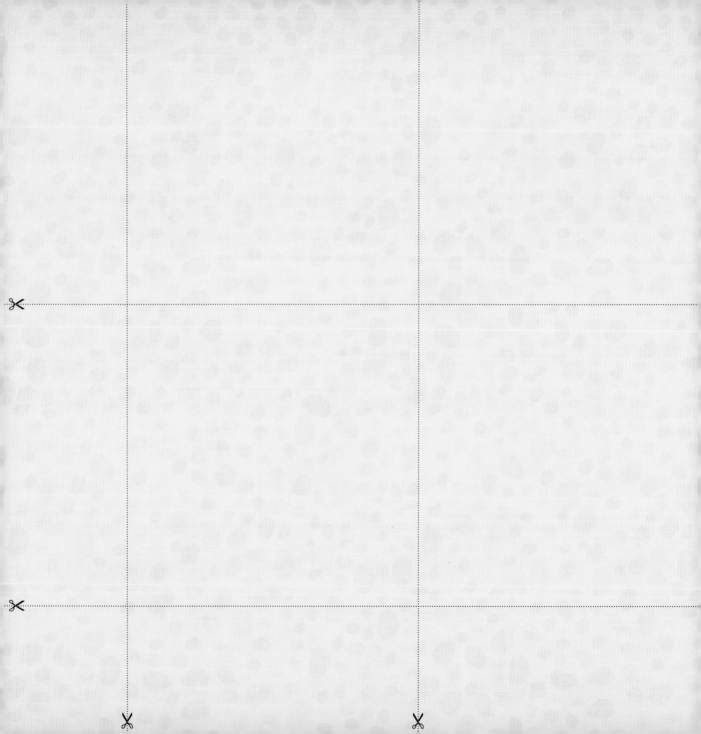

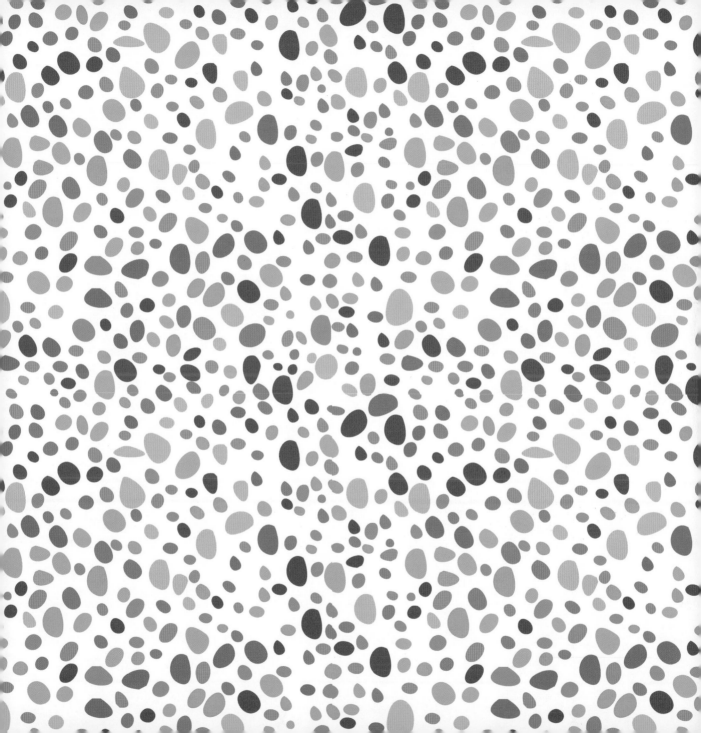

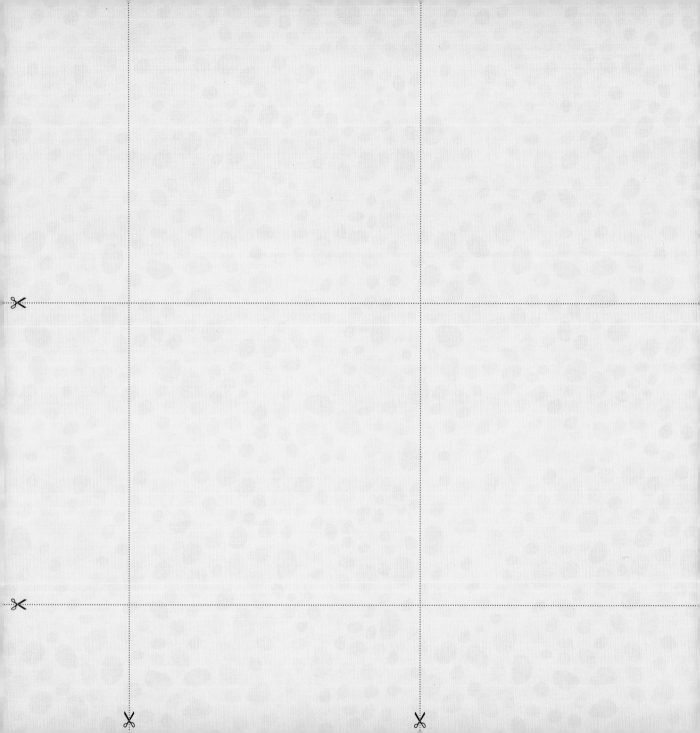

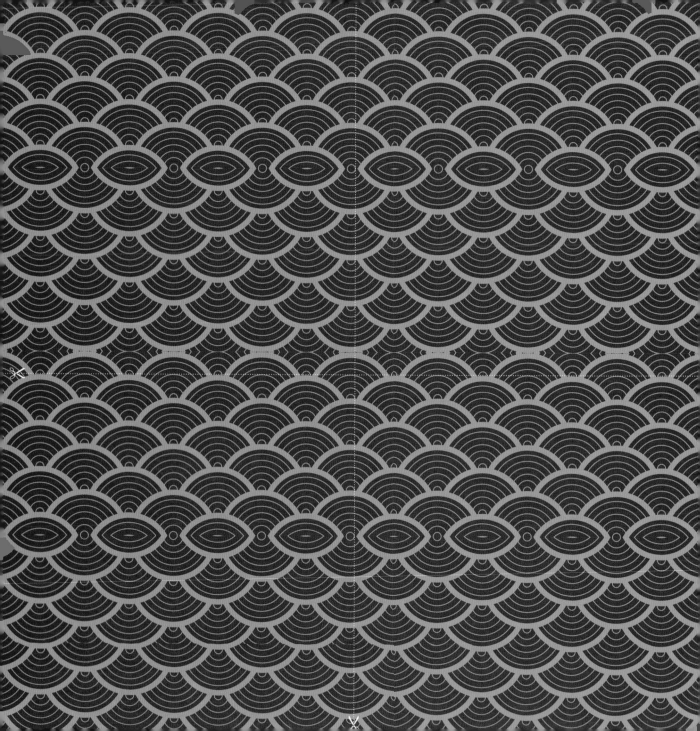

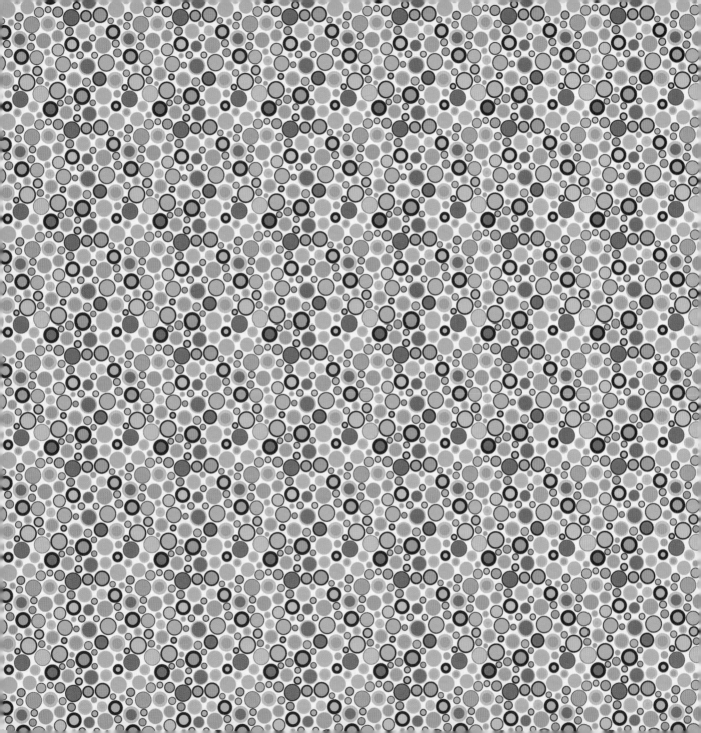

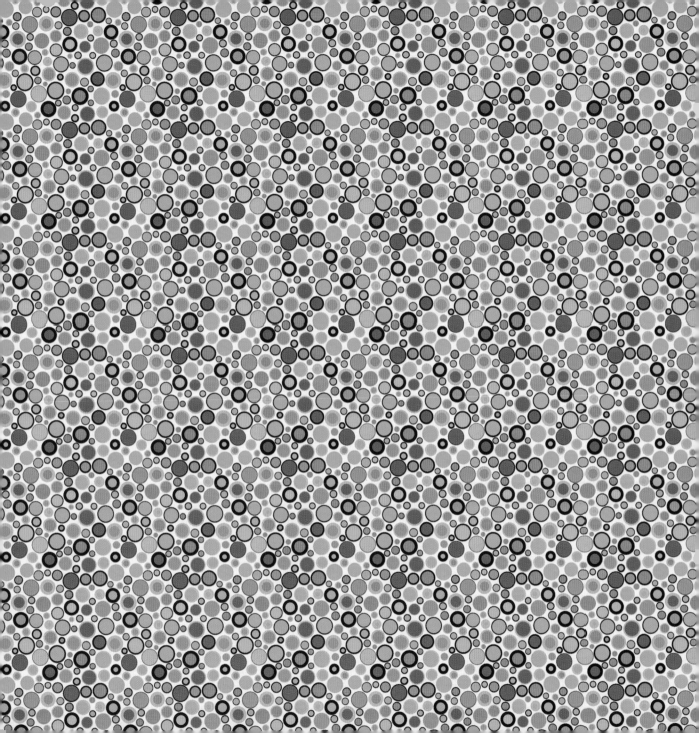

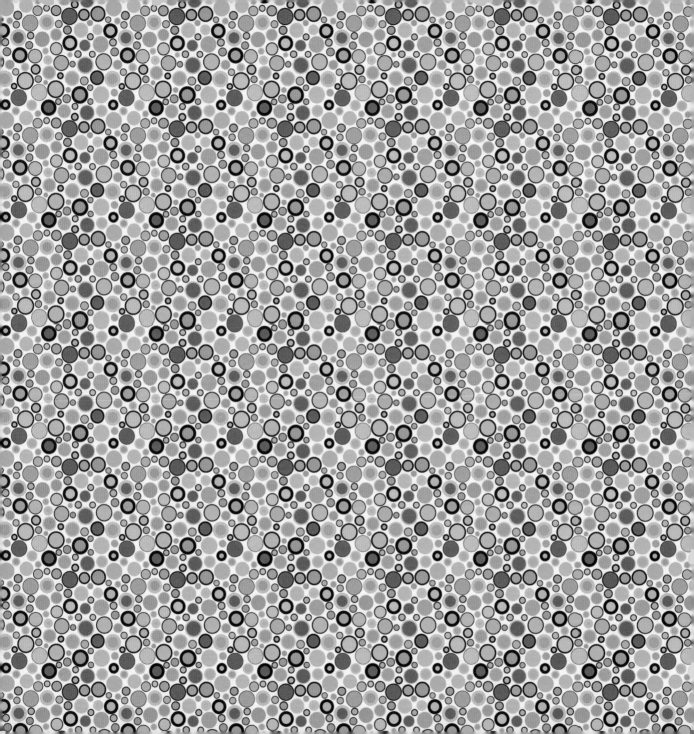

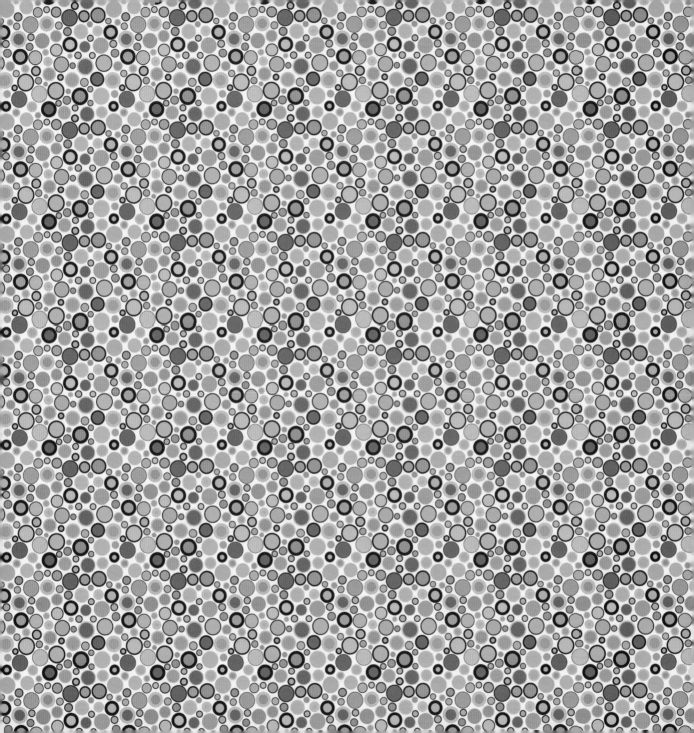

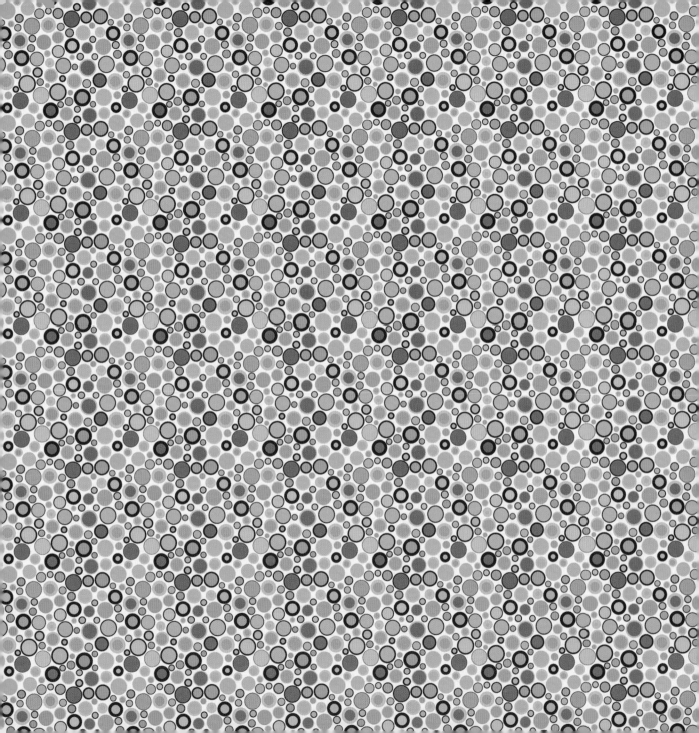

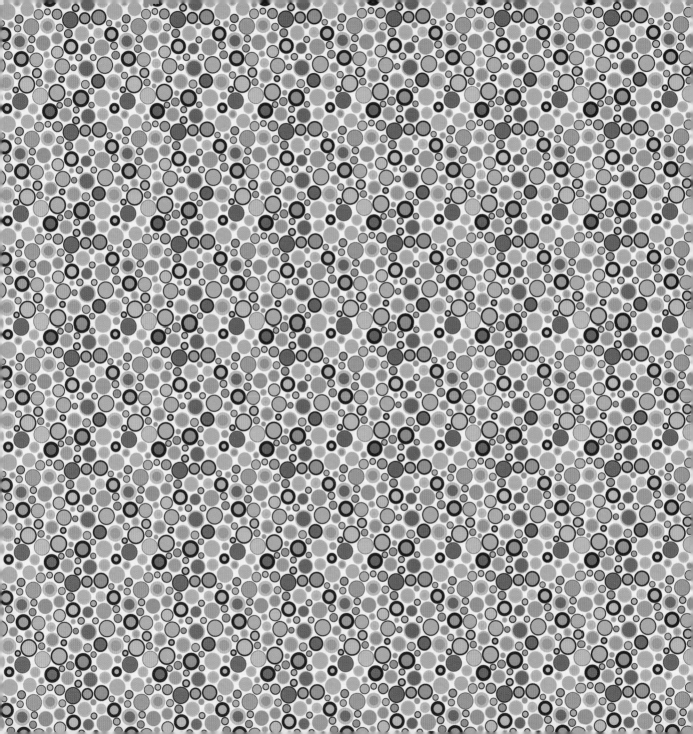

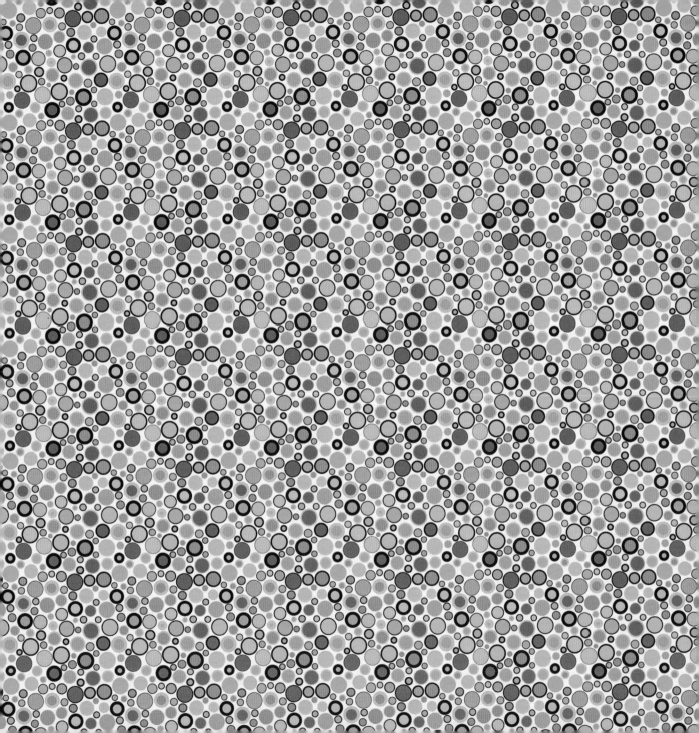

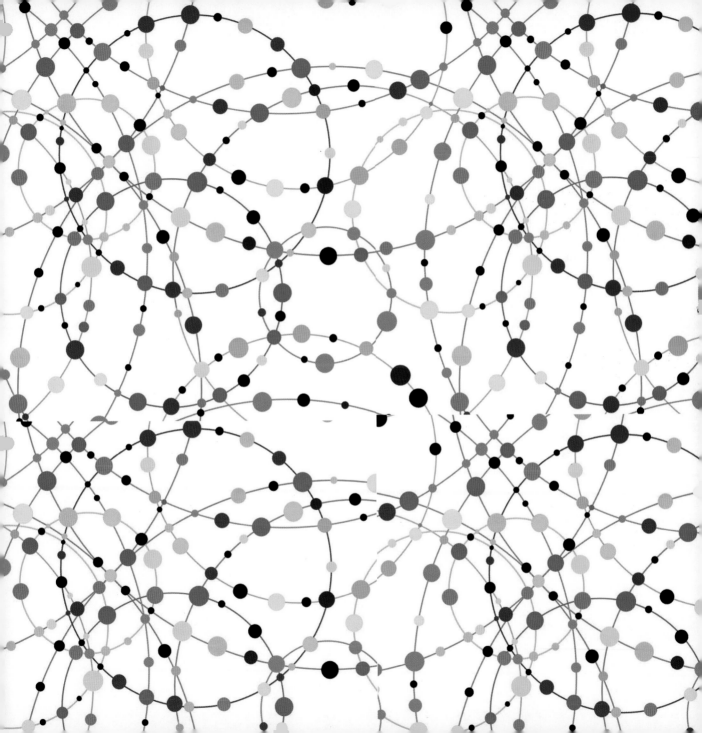

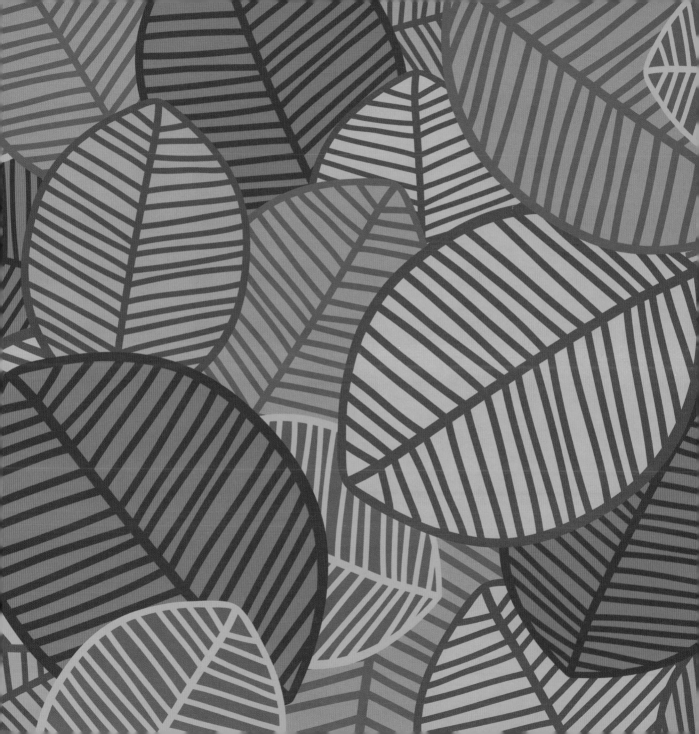

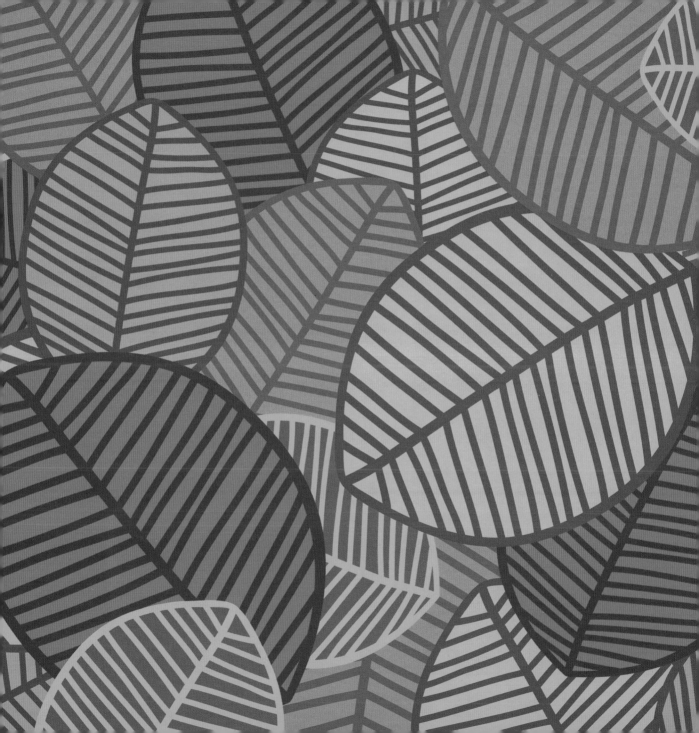

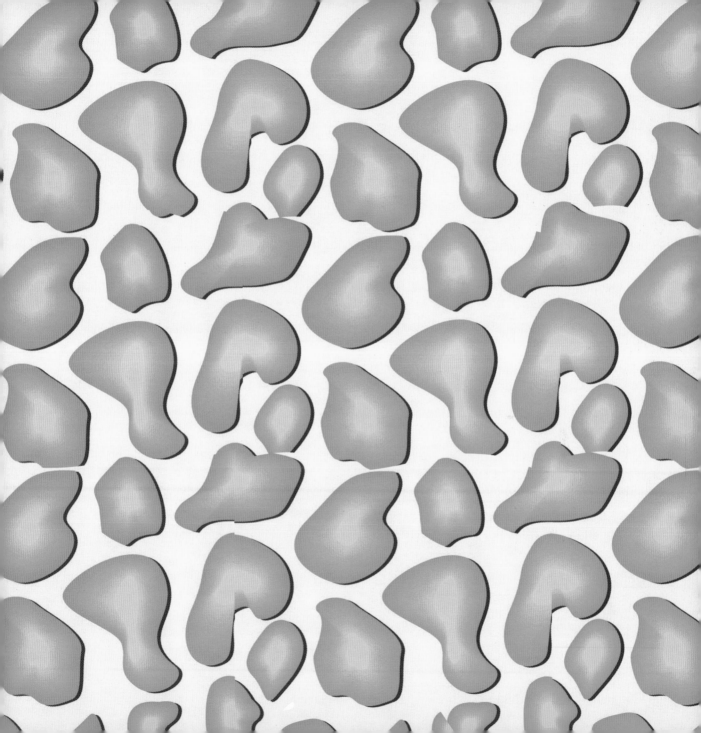

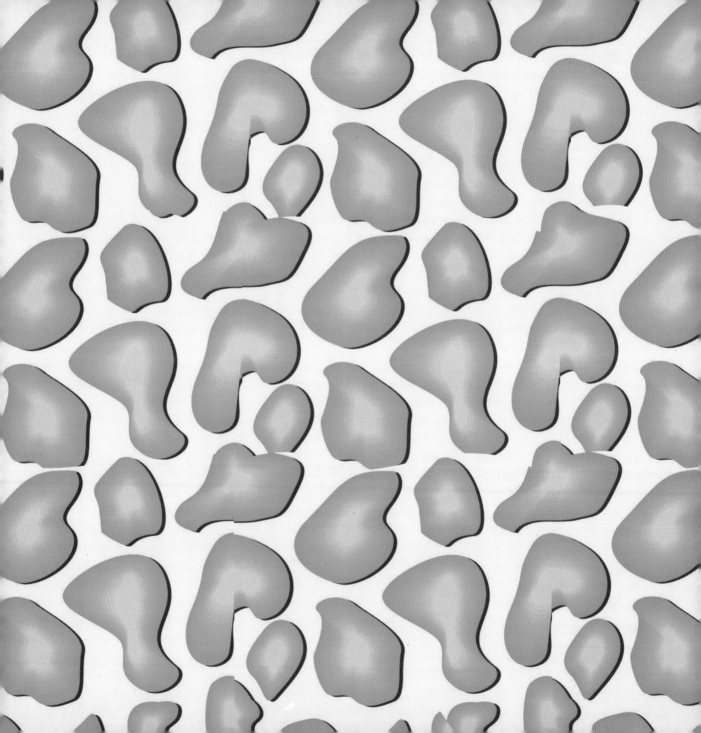

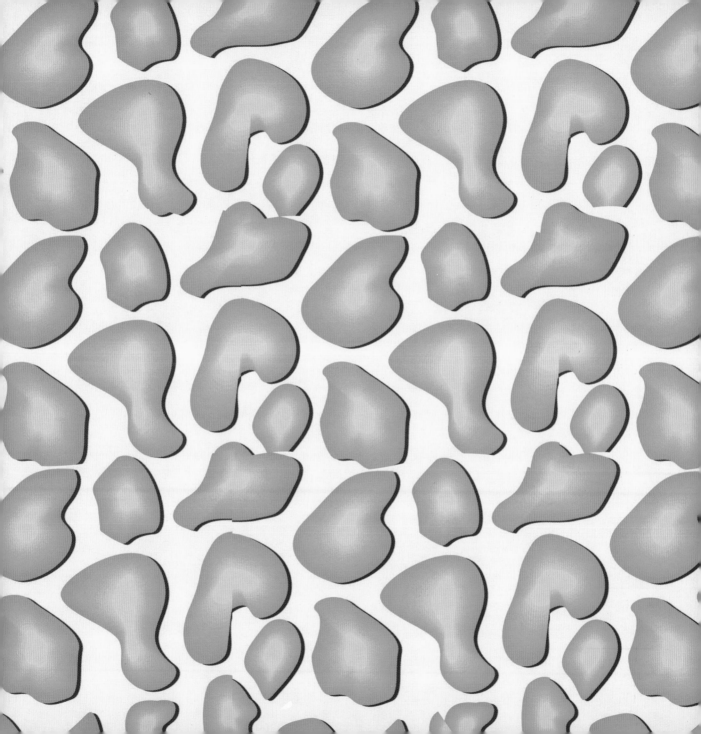

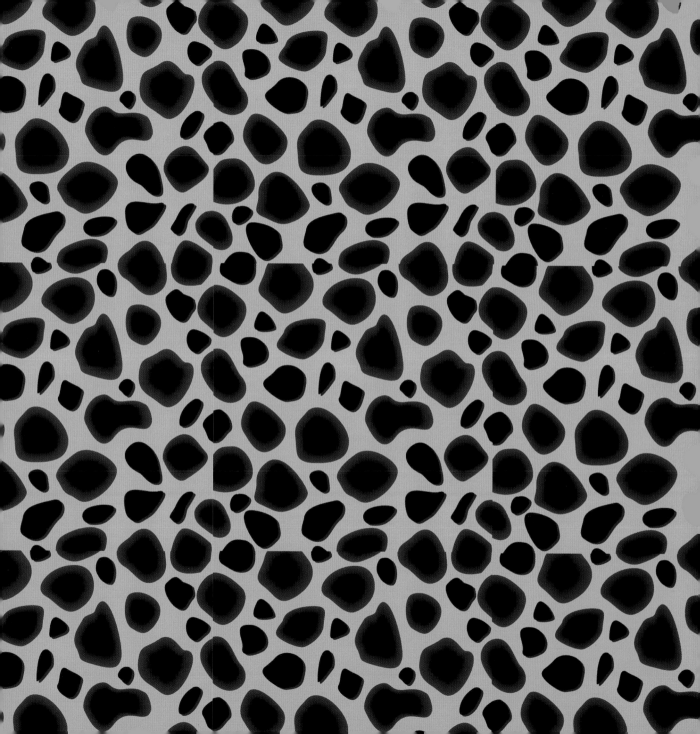

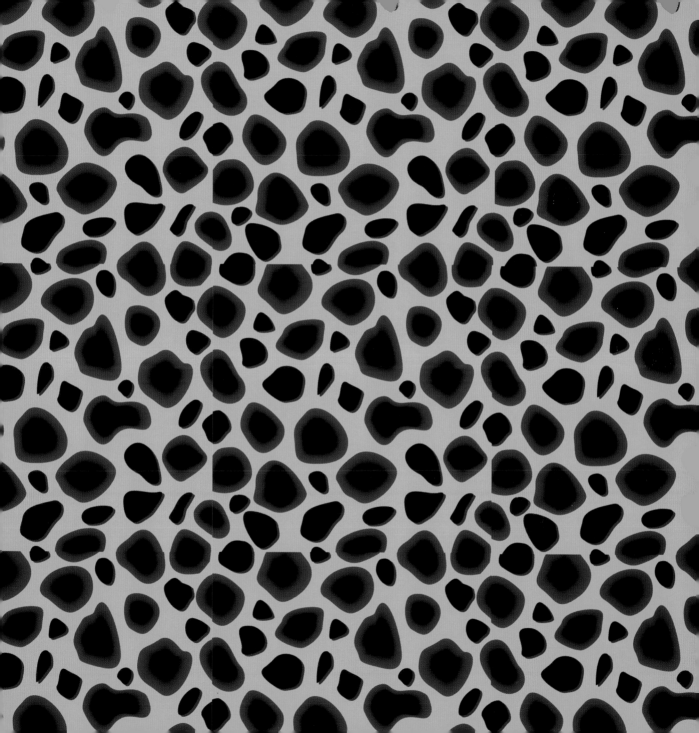

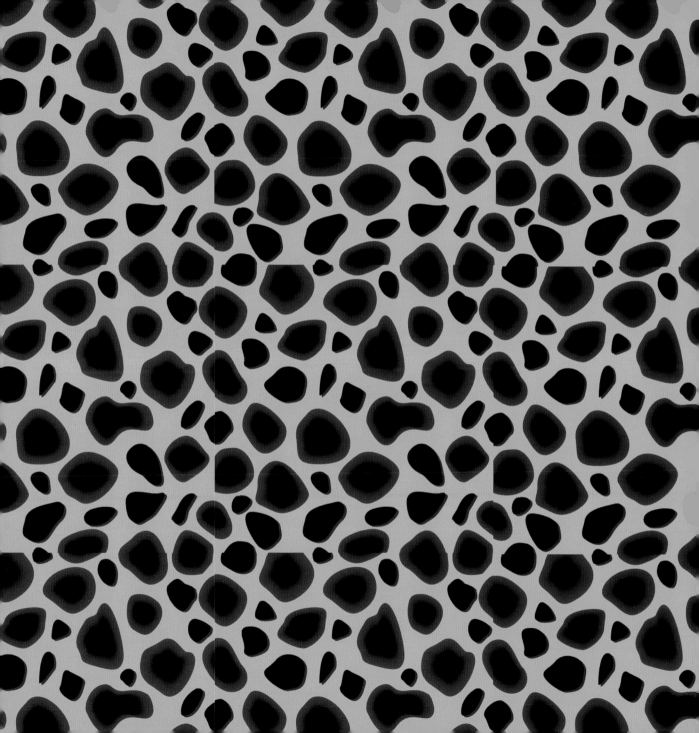

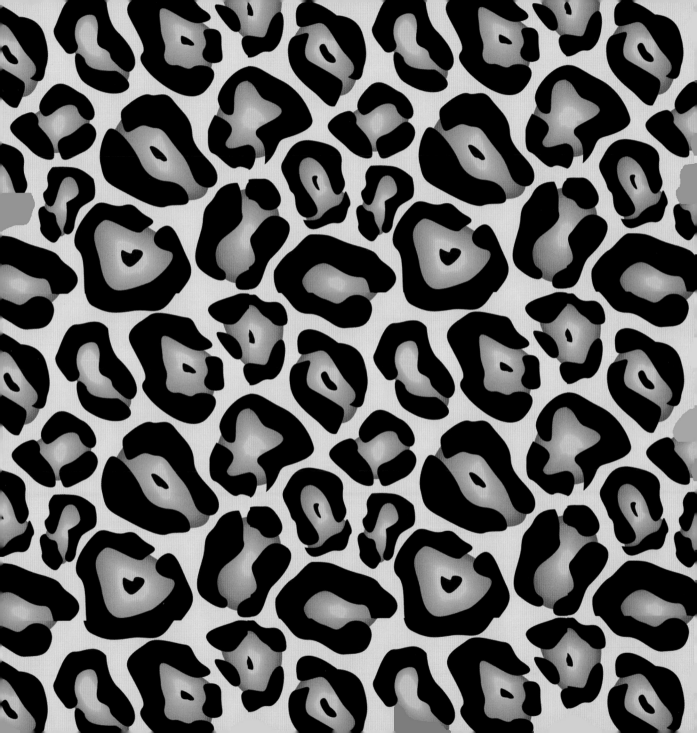

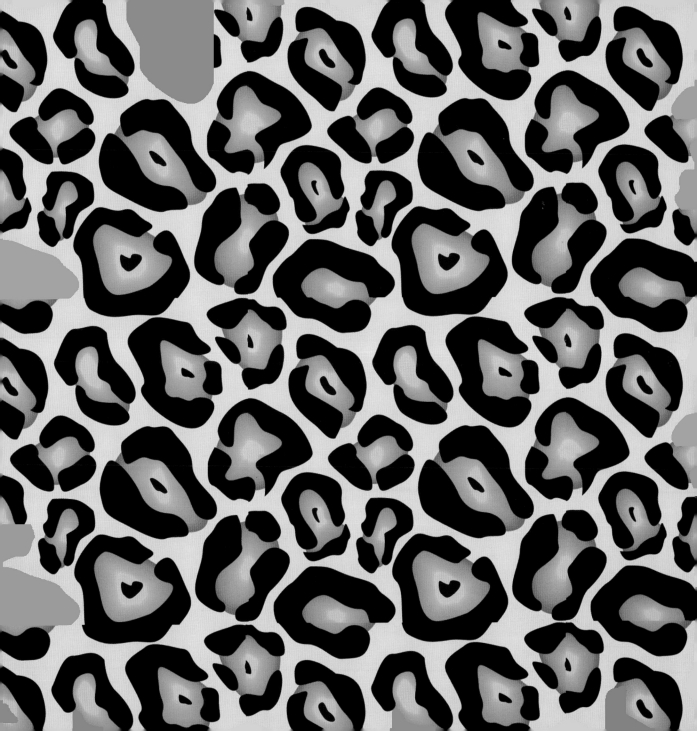

I love you
I LOVE YOU
I love you
I love you
I love you
I LOVE YOU
I love you
I love you
I LOVE YOU
I love you
I love you
I love you
I LOVE YOU
I love you
I love you
I love you
I love you
I LOVE YOU
I love you
I love you
I love you
I love you
I love you

I love you
I LOVE YOU
I love you
I love you
I love you
I love you
I love you
I LOVE YOU
I love you
I love you
I love you
I love you
I LOVE YOU
I love you
I love you
I love you
I love you
I love you
I love you
I love you
I LOVE YOU
I love you
I love you
I love you
I love you
I love you
I LOVE YOU
I love you
I love you
I love you
I love you
I LOVE YOU
I love you
I LOVE YOU
I love you

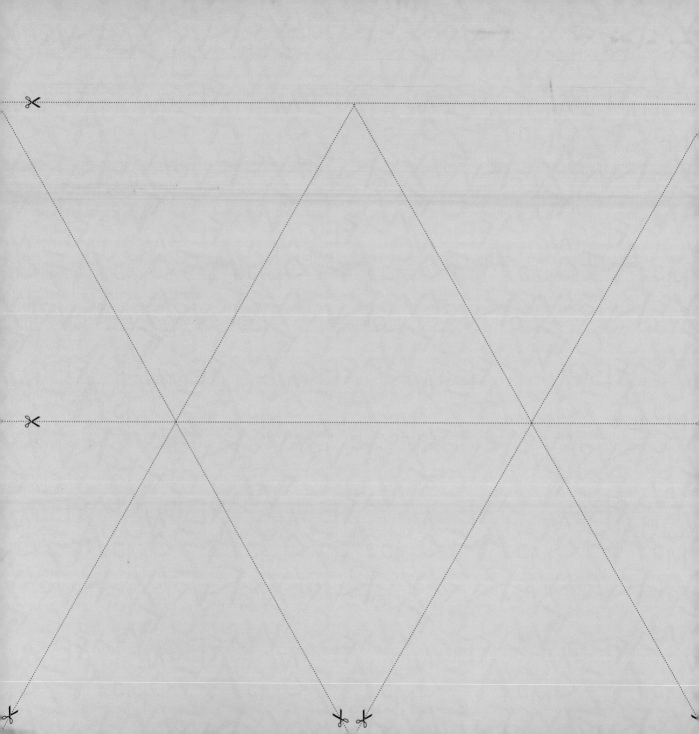

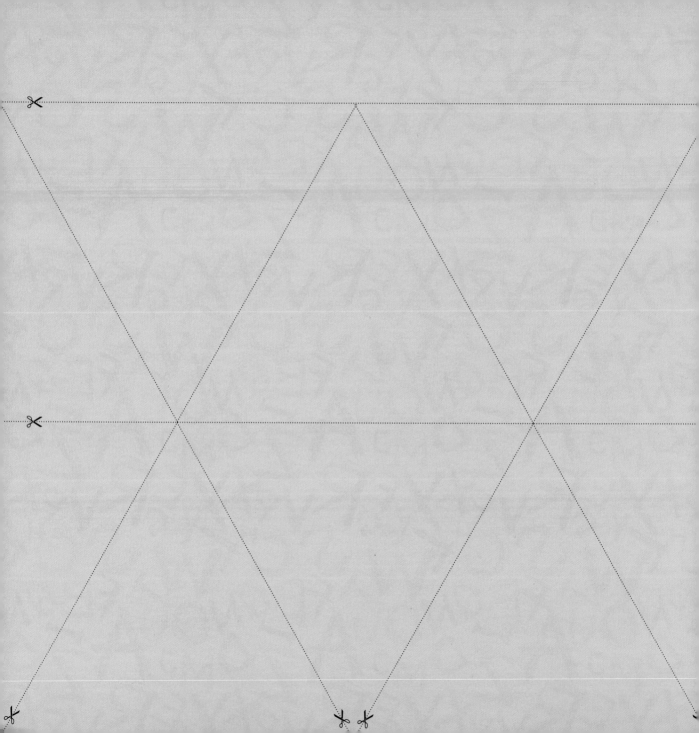

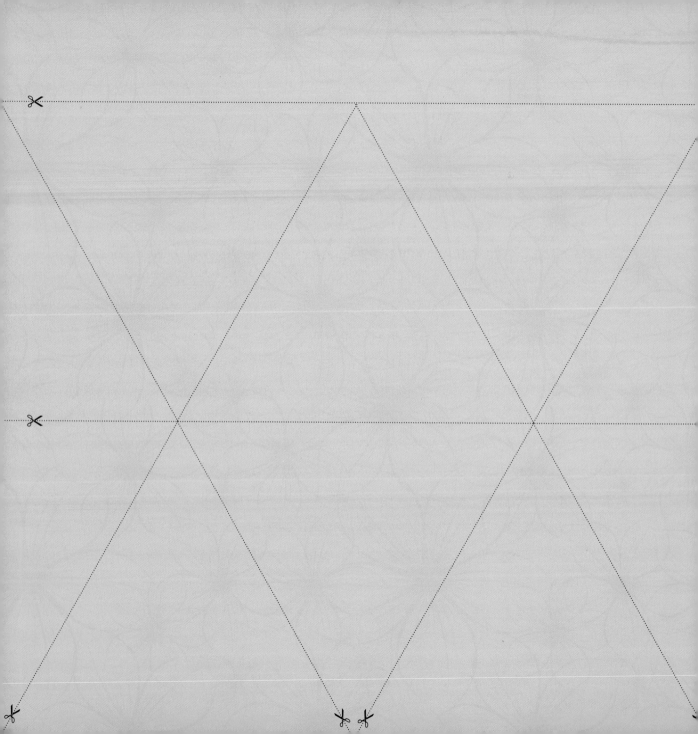